SYSTEMS THEORY
AND
FAMILY THERAPY

A Primer

Second Edition

Dorothy Stroh Becvar
Raphael J. Becvar

University Press of America,® Inc.
Lanham • New York • Oxford

University Press of America,® Inc.
4720 Boston Way
Lanham, Maryland 20706

12 Hid's Copse Rd.
Cumnor Hill, Oxford OX2 9JJ

Library of Congress Cataloging-in-Publication Data

Becvar, Dorothy Stroh.
Systems theory and family therapy : a primer / Dorothy Stroh
Becvar, Raphael J. Becvar.—2nd ed.
p.   cm.
In the first ed. Raphael J. Becvar's name appears first on the t.p.
Includes bibliographical references and index.
1. Family psychotherapy. 2. Social systems. I. Becvar, Raphael J.
II. Title.
RC488.5.LB39   1998   616.89'156—dc21   98-46481 CIP

ISBN 0-7618-1295-4 (pbk: alk. ppr.)

To Lynne and John Reif,
very important members
of our family system

CONTENTS

ACKNOWLEDGMENTS

In this second edition we continue to give thanks to those individuals, couples and families with whom we have worked and whom we have endeavored to help to experience happier lives. We also give thanks, once again, to our students, trainees and colleagues whose provocative questions pushed us to think more clearly and to present our ideas in a clear and understandable manner.

INTRODUCTION: HOW TO USE THIS BOOK

> ....each man contemplates in his own personal way the stream of events upon which he finds himself so swiftly borne.
>
> George Kelly

This book is designed to be used as an introduction to a systems epistemology, or worldview. It does not pretend to be an all inclusive work. Rather, it seeks to provide basic learning to stimulate the reader to learn more about systems, about families, and about family therapy.

The reader is forewarned that we do not present the systems perspective. We present a systems perspective --our perspective. We describe some of the basic constructs by means of which social systems, and particularly the family, may be understood and we the challenge the reader to use this information to build his or her own theory about systems. This, we feel, one cannot not do. Indeed, it is highly unlikely that any person ever totally comprehends or understands a theory in exactly the same way as any other person. You may have your comprehension of a theory, but it probably is not the same understanding as that of its author. As we read any theory, we experience the meaning of its constructs and concepts consistent with and dependent upon the framework of concepts we have already learned and according to which we view the world.

The illustrations and examples provided in this book as we seek to explain concepts are based on the family as the social system of greatest interest to us. We could have used other social systems as examples. However, a more general application was not our purpose. You may find the concepts useful as you seek to understand other systems, but we leave that application to you.

Since first writing this book, much has happened both in the field of family therapy and in the evolution of systems thinking. Accordingly, in Chapter 2 we have extended our definition of systems theory to include cybernetics and describe the ways in which first-order cybernetics is consistent with modernism while second-order cybernetics and the related concepts of constructivism and social constructionism are more consistent with postmodernism. In Chapters 3 and 4 we define the various constructs and shifts in meaning that occur as one moves within cybernetics from the first-order level to the second-order. In Chapter 5 we discuss family interpretive systems as stories which participate in the creation of reality. In Chapter 6 we consider both traditional models of family development and in terms of a dynamic process model. In Chapter 7 we discuss the family as a system which requires consideration of the larger context if it is to be fully understood. The critiques and defense of a system perspective which comprise Chapter 8 have been expanded to include concerns about and support for both a systemic perspective in general and second-order cybernetics in particular. In Chapter 9 we continue to describe some general propositions and ideas which we have inferred from our systems perspective from the vantage point of an additional ten years of experience. You might consider these propositions and ideas as you build your own model for working with families.

Marriage and family therapy as an activity has legitimacy only from a perspective that sees people as interdependent. Our bias is that it makes no sense to do marriage or family therapy if one sees people as independent agents. A systems perspective provides a way of understanding the dynamics of this interdependence. What is more, it is a way that we have found to be very useful. It is our hope that you will find it useful as well.

Dorothy S. Becvar, Ph.D.
Raphael J. Becvar, Ph.D.
St. Louis, MO

Chapter 1

ABOUT THEORIES

> To be accepted as a paradigm, a theory must seem better than its competitors, but it need not, in fact never does, explain all the facts with which it can be confronted.
>
> Thomas Kuhn

To examine the developmental history of human societies is to learn of the many different ways in which people have attempted to explain the phenomena in their worlds. Kelly (1955) describes all people as scientists seeking to understand, predict and control their worlds. While this certainly may be useful, Berrien (1968) speaks of mankind's interminable need to make sense out of experience by raising it to ever higher levels of abstraction as an "incurable disease." Certainly the different explanations or theories offered and employed have each lead to courses of action different from those indicated by prior explanations or theories. For example, the explanation of the world as flat discouraged self-conscious attempts to sail around it. The explanation of "mental illness" as possession by demons suggested responses such as prayer, flagellation, or exorcism. The course of action we take is bound up with the explanation or meaning we experience when we encounter an event. Different explanations produce different interpretations and feelings which interact with different kinds of responses.

While the meaning we experience is a functional "truth" for us, we are always reminded that the same event can be given many interpretations. We typically select the interpretation which we believe will best serve our purposes. Such an explanation is derived from our personal frame of reference and thus tends to validate the theory. A person who believes that people are weak will have a predisposition to look for evidence of weakness in others. Accordingly, we are usually able to accept a different theory which invalidates our prior explanation only in the face of overwhelming evidence to the contrary.

Each of us has a variety of personal theories we use to explain physical, biological and interpersonal phenomena. Our personal theories are our guides as we move toward greater meaning and satisfaction in our lives. However, such guides are maps; they are not the territory (Bateson, 1972). We prefer to think of theories as stories in order to remind us that while they may be useful and thus true in some way, we cannot speak of them as Truth in an ultimate sense. Indeed, most of us are aware of certain inadequacies in our personal theories. Therefore, we often seek different, richer, or more detailed maps or stories.

This book focuses on the family and offers a theory, or map, or story, for your consideration. This theoretical perspective is derived from General System Theory (Bertalanffy, 1968) as it has evolved in the context of an attempt to understand the dynamics of families. A systems perspective has demonstrated its efficacy in the physical, biological, and social sciences; its application to the study of human beings has been equally fruitful.

To many social scientists, systems theory seems better than its rivals, for it can explain and predict events and solve problems recognized by clinicians as acute. That the systems perspective has come into its own is indicated by the growing number of professional journals and societies concerned with this topic as well as by inclusion in university curricula. Marriage and family therapy, which is built on a systems perspective, is now recognized as a separate mental health profession and it practitioners have achieved regulation in most of the states.   According to Kuhn (1970), these may all be considered characteristic of a paradigm shift.

There are many explanations for the emergence of systems theory as a new paradigm. Minuchin has offered an explanation which we find useful:

> Psychoanalysis is a nineteenth century concept...   Its the product of a romantic idea of the hero and his struggle against society; it is about man out of context.   Today we are in a historical period in which we cannot conceive of non-related things. Ecology, ethology, cybernetics, systems, structural family therapy are just different manifestations of a concern for the relatedness of our resources. Family therapy will take over psychiatry in one or two decades because it is about man in context.   It is a therapy that belongs to our century, while individual therapy belongs to the nineteenth century. This is not a pejorative. It is simply that things evolve and change, and during any historical period certain ways of looking at and responding to life begin to crop up everywhere. Family therapy is to psychiatry what Pinter is to theaters and ecology is to natural science. (Malcolm, 1978, p. 76)

However, despite its growth and greater acceptance, systems thinking is still not a part of the mainstream worldview of our society. While this may make learning its constructs somewhat challenging, it also may explain part of its utility in working with families. But more about that in Chapter 2.

Chapter 2

SYSTEMS THEORY/CYBERNETICS: A PARADIGM SHIFT

> The theory will have shown its value if it opens new perspectives and viewpoints capable of experimental and practical application.
>
> Ludwig von Bertalanffy

At base, the concept of a system is an invention which is used to describe regularities or redundant patterns we observe between people and other phenomena. Thus, systems exist in the eye of the beholder, only as we give them existence by observing regularities or patterns. To conceptualize a given pattern of relationships as a system is useful and simplifies our understanding of the world

Let us emphasize again our belief that the concept of a system, systems theory, or a systems perspective is, like all other theories, merely a map, or story, and does not necessarily describe the territory, or reality. The questions that are allowed, and thus the answers we obtain, are controlled by what our theory frames for us to describe. Indeed,

> Problems that remain insoluble should always be suspected as questions asked in the wrong way, like the problems of cause and effect. Make a spurious division of one process into two, forget that you have done it, and then puzzle for centuries as to how to get the two together. (Watts, 1972, p.53)

Systems theory is a unifying theory, and as such, represents a paradigm shift in terms of how we understand human behavior. Instead of studying objects and people discretely or in isolation, we now have a means of studying them in relationships. Along with the other systems we have invented, e.g., the solar system, society culture, neighborhoods, bureaucracy, we have also found it quite useful to construe the family as a system.

The systems perspective would have us see each member of a family in relation to other family members, as each affects and is affected by the other persons. According to systems theory, it makes no sense to analyze any person independently. To understand each person in a family, one must study how each is in relation to every other family member. To study a single member apart from the others, out of the context of family relationships, is to know that person relative to the new context (the context in which he or she is studied) but not in the context of his or her family.

If a person is studied in isolation, then the inquiry must be concerned with the nature of the individual. If the field of inquiry is expanded to include the interaction of behaviors and the context in which these behaviors occur, the focus shifts from the isolated monad, which does not exist within systems theory, to the relationships between the parts of a system. From a systems perspective, the observer of human behavior turns from an inferential study of the mind to the observable manifestations of relationship.

Since the components of a human system such as a family are interrelated, it follows that each family member's behavior cannot be viewed and treated as an isolated unit. Rather, all behavior must be considered relative to context, as both antecedent and subsequent to the behaviors of other family members. All events in a family must be considered simultaneously as subsequent and antecedent behaviors.

To be consistent with the systems perspective, we must use the same framework to view families in general. That is, the family as a system is a component, or subsystem, of a larger network of systems, the suprasystem. Therefore, to understand each family, one must study how that family is in relationship with other families in their broader societal and cultural contexts. As individuals within a family interface and interact with one another, so families interface and interact with other families as well as with other systems. Just as an individual is studied in the context of his or her family, so the family is studied in the context of its environment.

The systems perspective, therefore, moves us away from linear cause-effect thinking, i.e., that A influences B but B does not influence A, as in the following examples:

"I treat you like a child because you behave like a child."

"I behave like a child because you treat me like a child.

With a systems perspective we are moved to a reciprocal or circular notion of causality, i.e., A and B are in dynamic interaction, as illustrated below:

"When I treat you like a child, you behave like a child, and then I treat you like a child even more and you behave even more like a child. We sure have a vicious cycle going, don't we."

"When I behave like a child, you treat me like a child, and then I behave like child even more and you treat me like a child even more. We are sure caught up with each other, aren't we."

From a systems perspective, our view of reality would have us perceive with Bronowski (1978) a "constantly conjoined universe" in which ultimate knowledge, or truth, is not accessible to us. Rather, given the assumption of total interconnectedness, we now think in terms of theoretical relativity. According to this concept, good and bad are understood to be inherent in all frameworks but there is no one absolute good. Each theory is thus evaluated in terms of its usefulness in a given context.

The notions of interdependence and relationship entail our understanding individuals and families in mutual interaction and in the context of their environments. Causality becomes a reciprocal concept to be found in the interface between individuals and systems. Responsibility exists only as a bilateral process. As different as all this may seem, however, there is much about systems thinking that remains consistent with a modernist perspective.

Modernism

Modernism, as well as the related perspective of structuralism, is associated with a realist epistemology according to which one assumes it is possible to achieve objective knowledge of the world. From this perspective one seeks universal codes, structures, and essences which are assumed to exist "out there" independent of observers. The goal is to discover, map, and know objectively the truth of the world of human behavior.

The modernist perspective provides the foundation for the traditional mental health practice and research in which the characteristics of healthy and unhealthy, functional and dysfunctional, normal and abnormal individuals, couples and families are studied. A modernist seeks universal truths which are believed to transcend differences in cultures and societies. Such truths are obtained through "systematic observation and rigorous reasoning" (Gergen, 1991, p. 29). Further, within the modernist tradition, language is considered to be representational, or to report what is "discovered" out there.

Such a view describes the world of the professional as expert, or social engineer, who takes charge of and sets the goals for therapy. This is the context in which diagnosis, treatment planning, and therapy for problems consistent with the various categories used to define dysfunctional couples and families makes sense. Accordingly, "The therapist seeks, discovers, and treats the 'real' problem, the underlying structural flaw that is built into the system and which necessarily gives rise to symptoms" (Becvar & Becvar, 1993, p. 142). Further, an important part of the social engineering thrust of modernism is the socialization of people into an almost worshipful attitude toward science. That is, professionals suggest that living, parenting, marriaging, and familying should not be trusted to the untrained. Rather, according to the myth of professionalism, consumers are encouraged to look to the experts for knowledge and guidance regarding how to live their lives. It is assumptions such as these that are disputed by those espousing a postmodern perspective.

Postmodernism

Postmodernism, which first found expression in the fields of sociology, semiotics, literary deconstruction, and communication theory, challenges the idea as well as the possibility of objective knowledge and absolute truth. By contrast, it is assumed that our "reality" is inevitably subjective, thus calling into question at a fundamental level the search for universal codes, structures, and essences. From a postmodern perspective it also is assumed that people live in a reality comprised of socially constructed and socially sanctioned narratives, or stories. Further, rather than inhabiting a universe, it is understood that we dwell in a multiverse. This multiverse, or context of multiple perspectives, is created through the act of observation and use of language in which everyone participates. Postmodernism also challenges the idea of therapists and social scientists as the possessors of expert knowledge. Alternatively, it is understood that clients and professionals have equally valid perspectives and that each person is the possessor of his or her own expertise. Indeed, it is acknowledged that the idea of professionals as the sole possessors of "expert knowledge" legitimizes the practice of social engineering and necessarily disempowers consumers given that the possession of expert knowledge and power are inseparable (Foucault, 1979). It is recognized that rather than having facts, all we have are our various perspectives and thus our attention must shift to language and the role of discourse. Language and the role of discourse are the focus of both constructivists and social constructionists, although their emphasis varies somewhat as is described in the following two sections.

Constructivism

> For the postmodernist, language is understood as the means by which individuals come to know their world and in their knowing simultaneously to construct it. (Becvar & Becvar, 1996, p. 88).

That is, those espousing a constructivist perspective believe that in the process of perceiving and describing an experience, whether to ourselves or others, we construct our reality as well as our personal knowledge base about reality. It is we who through our beliefs discern the way things are. In other words, believing is seeing. Thus, the idea that we can observe and can know the truth about people (as well as other phenomena in the world) in any objective way is deconstructed. Rather, we assume that all we can know are our constructions of people and other world phenomena.

From the perspective of constructivism, we see knowledge as actively constructed by the individuals who are doing the knowing. While a real reality somewhere out there is not denied by such a stance, the possibility of a "true" representation of that reality is denied. The individual, including the social scientist and the mental health professional, can only know his or her constructions of others and the world. And such constructions are expressed through a system of language which is understood to have a separate existence. Understanding the context of language as well as its creation and ramifications moves us into the realm of social constructionism.

Social Constructionism

For the social constructionist, language is not a reporting device for our experience, or representationalism. Rather it is a defining framework for our experiences. Thus a change in language equals a change in the experience for the social constructionist believes that reality cannot be experienced directly. What is more,, the reality experienced is inseparable from the prepackaged thoughts of the society, or what have been referred to as "forestructures of understanding" (McNamee & Gergen, 1992, p. 1).

To explain, each of us is born into a given sociocultural context and as we learn the language of our group we internalize the norms, values and ideology of this context. We come to speak in terms of the universal conventions, metaphors and symbols by which our community is characterized. According to Watts, "our most private thoughts and emotions are not actually our own. For we think in terms of languages and images which we did not invent, but which were given to us by society" (1972, p. 64). And knowledge as narratives embedded in cultural stories is never final; it is always negotiable.

From a social constructionist perspective a primary goal is to deconstruct so-called facts by delineating the assumptions, values and ideologies upon which they rest. We also are admonished to consider ourselves and our constructions about life and living with skepticism and perhaps humor. For we recognize that the self, with all of its attendant problems, is constructed in relationship. The individual is understood to be a participant in multiple relationships. Further, a problem is only a problem as a function of the way it is constructed in certain relationships. That is, there are no decontextualized individuals or problems. Accordingly, great importance is given to the role of conversation, to an awareness of the co-construction of problems and proposed solutions and to the need for respect for individual differences.

Although individuals, couples or families may present for therapy, the unit of analysis involves those other people who are "in language" or "languaging" about the problem. It is understood that being "in language" or "languaging" about the problem participates in creating and maintaining the problem. Thus, it is appropriate to focus on the narrative according to which meaning is experienced. For meaning is not implicit in an experience. Rather, people have problems as a function of the way an experience is languaged, or interpreted, or classified, or categorized.

First-Order and Second-Order Cybernetics

As the concepts of systems theory were translated into the practice of family therapy, a paradigm shift was initiated. However, while seeing whole families and understanding people and problems in context certainly constituted a radical change from traditional mental health practice, for the most part the original family therapy models remained consistent with a modernist perspective (Becvar & Becvar, 1996). These models and the concepts upon which they are based generally fall into the category of what we refer to as first-order cybmernetics. The completion of the paradigm shift required the creation of approaches consistent with a postmodern perspective. These approaches are consistent with systems theory at the level of second-order cybernetics. In the next two chapters we shall attempt to further delineate the concepts which characterized a systems perspective at these very different levels.

Chapter 3

FIRST-ORDER CYBERNETICS: DEFINITIONS OF CONCEPTS

General System Theory is the skeleton of science in the sense that it aims to provide a frame work or structure of systems on which to hang the flesh and blood of particular disciplines and particular subject matters in an orderly and coherent corpus of knowledge.

Kenneth Boulding

Like all theories, systems theory has concepts and constructs which have meanings specific to the theory. From a systems perspective, you will find neither intrapsychic labels such as ego, self-concept, drive, self-awareness, etc., nor labels assigning internal motivation, such as the concepts of discounting, selfish, rescuing, etc., as descriptors of behavior. Similarly, the concepts of influence, control, purpose and goal are meaningless in the context of a perspective according to which systems (as elements of a larger, suprasystem) are understood to interface with other systems in an ongoing, mutually recursive manner.

In this chapter we define the basic constructs of systems theory and family therapy at the level of first-order cybernetics. However, before proceeding, it should be remembered that the phenomenon under study tends to interact with the theory that seeks to explain that phenomenon. So it is when we attempt to explain a systems perspective and use it to study the family. It is not that the theory is necessarily corrupted, but rather that we, as creative human beings, define according to our personal frames of reference the constructs and concepts which we use to describe that which we study. Thus the distinctions we make and the differences we observe are those we have created as a function of the theory or map we employ in an attempt to understand or explore our world and the people in it.

The definitions and explanations provided in this book are interpretations which we find useful in the study of families and as we work to help families through therapy or development and enrichment activities. If our explanations differ from others you may read, it is because we assume the same right to create as did the seminal theorists on whose work we build. We do not deprecate in any way the efforts or work of others; we merely reserve the right to describe our own interpretation--our own story about a systems perspective. Part of this story includes the distinction we make between first-order and second-order cybernetics.

From the perspective of first-order cybernetics, while the unit of concern moves from the individual to the family, or larger context, the observer remains outside the system. The observer as therapist attempts to understand what is going on within the family from a frame of reference that does not include him or herself. He or she also generally attempts to assess family interaction relative to a particular idea about how things should be. What is significant is the focus on patterns, relationships and process. This is done through a consideration of the following concepts which we have chosen for inclusion in this chapter:

Boundaries

Communication/Information Processing

Context

Entropy and Negative Entropy

Equifinality

Homeostasis, Morphostasis and Morphogenesis

Open and Closed Systems

Positive and Negative Feedback

Recursion

Relationship

Wholeness

Boundaries

A fundamental characteristic which we infer from our observations of systems is their boundaries. In the family system, this boundary is defined by the redundant patterns of behavior which characterize the relationships within that system and by those values which are sufficiently distinct as to give a family its particular identity. Family members are defined, and are thus able to be distinguished from other families and systems, by the information or communication which flows between them

Most people are members of several different systems. To some extent, each relationship within a particular system defines and is defined by the relationships in all the other systems of which one is a member. The amount of information permitted into a system from without, or out of the system from within, indicates the rigidity of the boundary, or the openness or closedness of a system.

If a family or other system accepts too much information from without, the boundaries of that system become indistinct and are not discernible as separate from other systems. On the other hand, if the boundaries are too rigid, the system will not be sufficiently flexible to effectively process information from its environment. The system must constantly interact with the environment in which it exists and boundaries are the means by which that system both accepts useful information and screens out information deemed unacceptable.

The concept of boundary implies a hierarchy of systems in which there is both separateness and connectedness. A family system is but one "defined" subsystem which is described as existing as a part of a larger system, or suprasystem. That is, the concept of boundaries connotes both the separateness of subsystems from each other and from a larger system and yet a belongingness of all parts to the whole. Similarly, each family is a unique system and is also a part of the system of all families. And relationship subsystems exist within the larger system of the family.

Maintenance of family identity involves a process in which the boundary functions as a buffer for information from outside the system, screening it for compatibility with the family value system. Similarly, when a family member considers the option of also becoming a part of another system, that system will be examined with an eye for discerning behavior patterns and values which are reasonably compatible with those of the family system. And a similar screening process will be employed by the other system as it considers the acceptance of the new member.

The boundary also describes the "exit" for information from a system. Such information is different from the inputs of other systems and is not purely what happened within the system. Rather, incoming information is transformed by the system and is then emitted as new information to other systems.

In summary, we define the boundary as that region through which inputs and outputs must pass, during which exchanges between systems and with their environment reflect a mutually interactive process (Berrien, 1968). Thus a boundary describes the possibility of energy or information transfer, in either direction, between all systems which interface in reasonable proximity to one another. However, as systems only exist in the eye of the beholder, it is important to remember it is we who infer the presence of boundaries as we observe the communication patterns within and between systems.

Communication /Information Processing

Communication patterns also define the nature of relationships in a family system. In an effort to understand these patterns, three levels of communication have been identified. These include the verbal,, also known as the digital mode, the non-verbal, and the context. The analogical mode is made up of the non-verbal and context levels.

Verbal communication refers to the explicit, the words or labels we use to transmit information. Also known as the report or *digital* mode, verbal communication is considered the least powerful element in defining the nature of a relationship or system: "Indeed, whenever relationship is the central issue of communication, we find that digital (verbal) language is almost meaningless" (Watzlawick, Beavin & Jackson, 1967, p. 63). For example, the explicit content of the sentence, "The garbage is piling up," is purely descriptive. Without specifying other aspects - the nonverbal and the context - of the relationship between speaker and listener, the probable response is non-specific.

Non-verbal communication refers to such things as voice tone, gestures, facial expression, body posture, inflection, etc. Non-verbal behavior is the command, or relationship-defining mode of communication. In effect, it tells the receiver of a message what to do with the message. The non-verbal mode is the part of the message that comments upon how the message is to be received, or the sender's meaning and intention. Thus the sentence, "The garbage is piling up," stated by a father to a son in the kitchen probably contains the indirect command, "Take the garbage out." Every non-verbal communication can be verbalized or made digital.

Context is closely associated with non-verbal communication and together these two modes comprise the *analog*. Typically, a change in context indicates a change in the rules of a relationship. Where we are, with whom, and when, all define how we relate, for example, with friends, at home, in church, etc. The context is capable of making the non-verbal verbal and it also subsumes or qualifies the non-verbal mode. The non-verbal, in turn, qualifies the verbal mode of communication, as illustrated below:

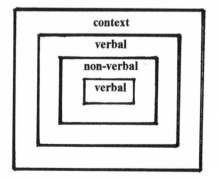

As noted, the statement, "The garbage is piling up," made by father to son in the context of the kitchen probably communicates the command, "Take the garbage out." However, the same verbal message spoken by father to son in the city landfill would have an entirely different meaning.

As a relationship (system) develops, its members consciously or unconsciously become sensitized to analog, to the implicit messages and meanings of their mutual interaction. Each person acts in a manner consistent with the nature of the relationship desired. The desired pattern of interaction emerges as a function of each person's belief system, which generally evolves in the context of his or her family of origin. Accordingly, reciprocal analogical signals are exchanged and tend to define the nature of the relationship.

Information flow is the basic process of a social system. Social systems are held together and change through the transfer of information/energy within and between the boundaries of different systems. Information/energy exchange implies a capacity for action and the ability to move toward either stability or change. However, to be useful, information/energy derived from both the characteristics and resources of members and from other systems must be organized; it must be neither random nor noise. With a high level of organized information flow, a system will move toward greater complexity, organization and an increased capacity to survive. That is, it will increase in negative entropy. Low level and disorganized information flow indicates movement toward entropy, a disorganized state characterized by a gradual but decreasing level of interaction between members.

In general, the lower the rate of the information flow, the more static and predictable, or entropic, a system becomes. On the other hand, a dynamic system is increasingly more unpredictable and marked by change as energy and power are shifted within. For human systems, this energy is the information flow, organized at higher and higher frequencies to enable the system to stabilize and/or adapt to change as necessary, and thus to continue its existence and maintain a state of negative entropy.

There are also three principles of communication to be considered as we seek to understand information processing within a system. These principles may be defined as follows.

Principle One. *One cannot not behave*. We do not have the choice of doing nothing so long as we live. Statements like, "I'm not doing anything," or, "I'm doing nothing," deny their own message and affirm the principle.

Principle Two. *One cannot not communicate*. All behavior in the context of others has message value. Indeed, even silence is a form of communication. Whether you intend to communicate or not, there is always a message implicit in every behavior or combination of behaviors you do. Thus, the statement, "We just don't communicate," describes perhaps dissatisfaction with how the speaker feels about the relationship, but there is communication. We have a choice to communicate verbally, but we have no choice except to communicate analogically. Those who observe you will interpret meaning relative to your behavior and your relationship to them.

Principle Three. *The meaning of a given behavior is not the "true" meaning of the behavior; it is, however, that individual's personal truth*. Any number of interpretations can be given to any set of behaviors. The way in which we define a behavior is thus associated with our previous experiences in similar situations and we make a fit between our beliefs, observations, and the events we experience. For many people, the meaning they experience constitutes for them the only meaning of an event rather than one among many possible meanings. Whatever meaning a person experiences in a given situation, it is probably that more credence is given to analogical messages than to verbal messages.

Context

Context was described above as being an essential aspect of the relationship-defining, or analogical, mode of communication. It was also mentioned that a change in context indicates a change in the rules of a relationship. Indeed, from a systems perspective we understand that change equals a change in context. We recognize that all behavior makes sense, or is logical, within a given context. Therefore, if there are behaviors with which people are unhappy, we attempt to facilitate change through a change in context. The goal is the creation of a new context within which the desired behaviors become logical and behaviors not desired no longer fit.

Entropy and Negative Entropy

All living systems are open to some degree. Although the degree of openness may vary, a living system always has some energy exchange with other systems in its environment. Entropy refers to the lack of energy or information in a system. Negative entropy, or negentropy, describes the tendency away from maximum disorder towards an appropriate state of order or balance. Input of new energy, which takes the form of information or communication between a system and other systems in its environment, is the basis of the negentropic trend in human systems like the family. That is, the family system accepts from other systems inputs that are necessary for its continued existence. While no family system is totally closed, in those more nearly closed, little new energy or information is being taken in. Nevertheless, in any system, entropy may increase, remain the same, or decrease. For all living systems are open and thus are capable of "intake of matter rich in high energy, maintenance of a high degree of order and even advancement..." (Bertalanffy, 1968, p. 159).

A family is constantly bombarded with input in the form of energy/information from other systems. In the process of retaining its identity as distinct from other system, it interacts with this energy input, processes it, and emits outputs to other systems which carry the family's distinctive mark. These outputs are energy transfers from the family to other systems which, in turn, may regard them as useful or useless (waste), i.e., not useful energy.

All systems need useful energy inputs to increase negative entropy. Without useful inputs, systems tend toward maximum disorder, or entropy. In such a state, the lack of structure or excess uncertainty may be defined as noise, or error.

A portion of the energy of a system is used to organize and maintain the system. Some energy is directed toward task functions. Too much energy directed toward maintenance functions at the expense of task functions, or vice-versa, can be problematic. For example, families can spend hours hassling over how to organize, how to organize to get organized, etc. Similarly, the family can go about the task of family life in a seemingly random and often conflictual manner, as little or no energy is directed toward maintenance functions. In a disorganized system the members lack a coherent sense of relationship and energy is expended thoughtlessly or in a random manner. The movement of the system at this point also is toward entropy. Balance is thus the key to achieving negentropy.

Equifinality

According to this construct, no matter where one begins, the ending will be the same. Put another way, there are many different paths to the same outcome. Literally meaning equal ending, equifinality has been defined as "The tendency towards a characteristic final state from different initial states and in different ways based upon dynamic interaction in an open system attaining a steady state" (Bertalanffy, 1968, p. 46). For example, in a conflictual relationship, regardless of variations in topic or content, the way that all subjects are debated tends to be the same.

The concept of equifinality precludes the need for an historical perspective, which some other psychological theories view as essential if therapy is to be successful. That is, with systems theory, the important question for the therapist becomes "what?" rather than "why?" The focus is on the here and now rather than on past history or the need for insight. The origins of a particular family situation are not considered to be nearly as important as is the organization of the ongoing interaction in that family at the present time.

The key is the pattern, and based on the notion of equifinality, we must observe the existing redundant patterns of communication or feedback processes in a given system. Indeed, in cases such as the conflictual relationship mentioned above, what is problematic are the attempted solutions, the repetition of patterns of communication that are not useful. The so-called "problem" is, in fact, maintained by repeated attempts to solve it in the same old (unsuccessful) way (Watzlawick, Weakland & Fisch, 1977).

In other words, the patterns of communication serve the function of maintaining the system in a steady-state around a problem. The dilemma is that an absolute steady-state in a system is probably not possible. Therefore, the problems tend to increase as a near steady-state becomes a part of the redundant pattern of communication.

Given the idea of equifinality, what you see is what you get, and that is all you need to know. Or, "The system is its own best explanation and the study of its present organization the appropriate methodology" (Watzlawick, Beavin & Jackson, 1967, p. 129). Thus, the way a family is interacting in the present provides the therapist with sufficient information to intervene effectively. Facilitating change within the system involves a focus on the family process as well as interaction with the here and now communication and feedback processes. This, in turn, impacts the structure and organization of the family.

Homeostasis, Morphostasis and Morphogenesis

Homeostasis is the construct which describes a system's tendency toward stability, or steady-state. Indicated by negative feedback, this state of dynamic equilibrium, or homeostatic balance, refers to the system's capacity to be stable. However, while useful, the concept of homeostasis is somewhat restrictive and misleading when applied to systems. A system seeks stability. Yet to continue to be healthy, it must also be able to change. Thus, the two related concepts of morphostasis and morphogenesis (Speer, 1970) were developed to augment the steady-state dynamic defined by homeostasis.

Morphostasis is similar in meaning to homeostasis with the addition of the fact that it connotes stability in the context of change. In other words, in order to be able to remain stable, a system must be able to change as appropriate. By contrast, morphogenesis delineates the system-enhancing behavior that allows for growth, creativity, innovation and change, which are all characteristics of functional families. However, it also connotes change in the context of stability inasmuch as stability is required in order for the system to be able both to change and to maintain itself.

In a healthy family system, morphogenesis (change) and morphostasis (stability) are both necessary. Thus there is a tendency in a relationship or a system to offset differences exhibited by one of the members. While either extreme of the morphogenesis-morphostasis continuum would probably be dysfunctional, in healthy families, a balance will be maintained between the two. That is, the rules of the system will allow for a change in the rules governing the system.

There are many times when morphogenesis is probably desirable. However, if change is permitted too frequently or to too great a degree, the stability of the family may be threatened. At the same time, the ability to change is also necessary as the family and its members grow and develop. For example, a child is not always five years old. If, as the child grows, the manner of parenting does not change in order to meet the demands of various developmental stages, the parent-child system may experience problems. Similarly, parenting a five year old with behavior appropriate for an older child is likely to be problematic. As Alfred North Whitehead notes, "The art of progress is to preserve order amid change and preserve change amid order."

The particular behavior patterns characterizing the relationships within a system define that system. When the system is functioning well, it will evolve as the characteristics of its members and their relationships change. Such changes do not disrupt the essential continuity of the system, and its continued existence is therefore assured.

Open and Closed Systems

Openness and closedness refer to the nature of the boundaries a family establishes around family members and between itself and other systems. The more input family members accept from other family members, or a family allows from other systems, the more it is an open system. Conversely, the less input permitted, the more closed. As with morphogenesis and morphostasis, in the well-functioning family, a healthy balance between the two extremes seems most desirable.

Input from within a family and from other systems often represents pressure to change. If not enough change is allowed to occur, a system is said to be closed, although, as we have noted, all living systems are open to some degree. If too much change is permitted, that system is said to be open to a fault. A system can experience problems as a function of being either too open or too closed. In the former case it loses its identity as a system distinct from other systems. In the latter case, it exists totally outside the sphere of other systems.

In a system that is functioning well, neither openness nor closedness is good *per se*. Rather, the appropriate degree of openness or closedness can only be decided relative to context. For example, in a hostile environment, maintaining a closed system may be the only way to assure continuation of that system. In general, however, if a system changes either too fast or not enough, it can be problematic. Thus, the governing rules of a system should allow for accommodation to gradual developmental growth pressures.

The ideal pace of change in a system is probably idiosyncratic to that system, as tempered by input from outside, which, in turn, is a response to output from the system. Further, it is unlikely that all members of a family system will value the same rate of change. That is, adolescents, reflecting the ever increasing input from other systems, may want more rapid change in the family system than that desired by their parents. Thus the parents of adolescents often act to modify or restrict the nature of the rate of change. Similarly, a wife who tries to alter the marital relationship in response to values derived from a women's group espousing assertiveness may find her husband closed to this new information. Yet, if the system is to function at an optimal level, change needs to be accommodated in some way, to some degree. The contract between parent and child that was effective when the child was younger probably will not work for the adolescent-parent relationship. And the marital relationship that existed prior to the wife's exposure to a feminist point of view will need to change in some way or the marriage may not survive.

Positive and Negative Feedback

Communication, or information flow, is the energy input and output of human systems. This communication can also be described as feedback about whether the product of a system is useful or not (waste). The usual form of feedback within and between human systems is comprised of communication as described earlier, i.e., verbal, non-verbal and context levels, or digital and analogical modes. Stated somewhat differently, they describe what was communicated, how, and where.

Feedback is responsive to and indicative of fluctuations within the system. Thus, if persons A and B have established a fairly stable relationship pattern, and if A behaves in a manner exceeding the acceptable limits of the relationship, (which is probably feedback that the existing contract is not satisfactory or that B's behavior exceeds acceptable limits), B may give feedback to A in an attempt to return to the steady-state of the previous relationship contract. In this way mutual influence and feedback occur in an ongoing pattern of reciprocal interaction.

In classical general systems terminology, negative feedback is a message that the output by another has reached some predetermined maximum level and is an indication to cut off or reduce the inputs. In other words, a steady-state has been achieved and is being maintained. Positive feedback is the reverse situation, indicating that the output is less than some maximum. The feedback loop signals that change has occurred and that more inputs are appropriate (Berrien, 1968). In other words, feedback provides information about the degree to which near steady-state functioning is being maintained and allows for the tempering of external variation that might otherwise lead to fluctuation. Feedback processes therefore serve to increase the probability of the survival of the system.

As one cannot not communicate, one cannot give feedback, at least analogically. Thus, in human systems, communication can be equated with feedback processes. Family members will want other family members to behave according to the feedback they give each other. And this feedback about behavior will correspond with what each person believes; it must be self-validating. That is, we communicate, or give feedback, consistent with our ways of thinking and believing. We interact with others according to our models of how we think we and they should be.

As noted previously, in a family a certain degree of stability is necessary, and feedback processes serve to promote the desired stability. However, stability may be promoted through an awareness of a need for change in response to changes in family members or circumstances. The feedback processes provide information about increases and decreases in behavior valued by the family system within a tolerable range of variation. For example, a family's feedback mechanisms may reflect the awareness of a need for an increase in outputs of ten year old behavior from a ten year old child, and a decrease in outputs of five year old behavior from the same child. Or, the family's feedback mechanisms may reflect the desire for a an increase in outputs of twelve year old behaviors in the fifteen-year old child. In the latter case, the feedback processes may not serve the system well over time.

In popular usage, the label "positive feedback," generally refers to praise or a similar behavior, i.e., positive reinforcement. "Negative feedback" usually refers to criticism or some form of harassment, i.e., positive or negative punishment. From a systems perspective, positive and negative feedback are defined quite differently and neither connotes a judgment of good or bad. Therefore, both praise and criticism can be either negative or positive feedback. Feedback is determined to be negative or positive only relative to context.

Positive feedback in systems terms is a message that change has taken place. It is also a recognition that such change has been accommodated by the system or family. Positive feedback is therefore a deviation-amplifying mechanism which indicates that system maintenance behavior has occurred in response to change. For example, grounding a child as a means of punishment for some unacceptable behavior may be positive feedback.

Negative feedback indicates that the status quo is being maintained. It thus performs a homeostatic, or morphostatic function. For example, praise is a form of negative feedback when repetition of the behavior that preceded it is forthcoming. If a behavior beyond the range of a family's tolerance occurs and is acknowledged by either praise or criticism, *this initial response is positive feedback*. From that point on, however, whether the behavior is praise or criticism, the repeated response is negative feedback, or an indication of maintenance of the status quo.

Many parents believe that criticism is an effective mechanism for producing behavior change. However, criticism (positive feedback) in response to a new behavior that is beyond acceptable limits may serve a deviation-amplifying function. Thus, the initial response to new behavior is important in families. Instead of a critical response to a new, undesirable behavior, a more useful response may be feedforward, or a redirection of the behavior to fit family values. To a fifteen year old who stayed out too late, this might take the following form: "Our rule is that you come home on time. We know how hard it is to tell your friends that you need to call your parents, but this is what we expect of you when you cannot return at the appointed time."

Feedforward is thus a request for a behavior that is desired but has not yet occurred: "Would you hold me?" instead of "You never hold me." Feedforward as an alternative to criticism can avoid reciprocal criticism, which is the logical response. That is, criticism begets criticism. However, it is foolish to criticize someone for criticizing someone.

The occurrence of a new behavior in a family may suggest that change is appropriate in order for the family to be stable in a useful way. For the fifteen year old mentioned above, it is natural to want to move toward more separation and independence and to have more frequent contact with persons outside the family system. Behaviors in search of greater freedom do and will occur. How a family defines the occurrence is the key, not whether it will or will not happen. To respond with arguing, criticism and an exchange of heated words followed by punishment can make the peer group appear even more attractive and may serve to build this pattern into the family.

Continued praise for twelve year old behavior as part of an ongoing negative feedback loop may participate in the creation of a context that defines expectations on the part of all concerned such that twelve year old behavior in an individual continues well into adulthood. Similarly, positive feedback, or the initial arguments and punitive response to staying out too late, may tend to remain in the system with increasing frequency and greater intensity. Thus negative feedback not only indicates that the status quo is being maintained, it also may serve to amplify existing patterns in a family.

Haley (1963) suggests that family problems generally emerge when a family needs to move to the next developmental stage but instead gets stuck. The appropriate use of feedback mechanisms coupled with an understanding of developmental stages of individuals and families may therefore go a long way towards preventing problems from arising. And awareness of feedback mechanisms may facilitate the achievment of solutions once problems have occurred.

Recursion

Recursion refers to the ongoing mutual influence and shared responsibility of the members of a relationship or system. As noted in Chapter 2, with a systems perspective we move away from the idea of linear causality to a notion of circularity or reciprocity. Thus, we also move away from the concepts of blame or guilt. Rather, we recognize that regardless of the state of our relationship with another person, we have created it together. Each person gets 50% of the responsibility, no more and no less.

Given the concept of recursion, we also recognize that designating the beginning of a sequence of events is arbitrary. All behaviors are preceded by other behaviors and it is we who make the particular punctuation about where things started (Keeney, 1983). Accordingly, we recognize that we can't know the cause of a particular situation other than as a shared process in which all involved participated. Once again, as with equifinality, the consideration of *why* something happened in terms of pointing a finger at a single person or event is not meaningful. All we can really know with any certainty is *what* is going on in the here and now and that the responsibility for the creation of the particular situation is shared. Also meaningful for the family therapist is knowledge about *how* the participants in the relationship would like things to be different.

Relationship

This construct describes the patterns of interaction between two or more individuals. It also describes the rules governing how one family member is with another or how the two relate to each other. The energy transmitted in a relationship takes the form of information exchange or communication, both verbal and analogical, between the participants.

When two people meet, they immediately exchange behaviors which define the nature of their relationship. In the initial contact, as well as in each subsequent contact, the behavior of each interacts with the behavior of the other as both continue the process of defining their relationship. Thus a relationship may be seen as a bargain or contract about how and under what circumstances each will exchange certain kinds of behavior with the other.   And as the interaction proceeds, each message exchange limits the number of possibilities for acceptable behaviors in that relationship (Watzlawick, Beavin & Jackson, 1967).

To explain, after a number of exchanges have taken place, a stable, redundant pattern of behavior emerges. It can then be predicted that each person will be a certain way with the other. Predictability, which is the logical product of redundancy, generates trust: "I know who you are and who I am with you; the way you are with me, the way I am with you."

It is the redundant patterns of interaction between and among family members which distinguish their system of relationships from any other system. These patterns may be called rules, and they usually exit outside the awareness of the people in a relationship. However, we may infer the rules of a relationship based on our observation of the regularities in these redundant patterns of interaction. Such implicit rules are the keys both to our understanding and to the definition of a particular relationship.   Although the participants may have certain explicit rules for their relationship, these tend to be of secondary importance to its definition.

The concept of relationship, therefore, refers to the rules which define its uniqueness, or to that which we infer when we observe members of a system exchanging redundant patterns of behavior with one another. Relationship thus denotes the interdependence described under Wholeness: It is the third part of the equation $1 + 1 = 3$.

The appropriate units of analysis in the study of human systems are the relationships between members and the organization or rules for these relationships. From intrapsychic psychology we have a rich vocabulary to describe individuals. For example, we have labels such as introverted, extroverted, dominant, submissive, kind, cruel, etc. However, in the relatively new application of systems theory to human behavior, we do not have the same richness of categories to describe the relationship patterns we observe. One of the few that has been described is symbiosis, which refers to the dependence for continuation of a particular behavior in one person upon the continuation of a particular behavior in another. Accordingly, the behaviors mutually feed and maintain each other.

Bateson (1972) provided an assist in the development of a relationship labeling system when he observed two distinctive patterns in native tribes during anthropological field studies. He termed theses relationships *complementary* and *symmetrical*. Watzlawick, Beavin and Jackson (1967) refined these concepts, which are defined as follows: A complementary relationship is one in which the interaction between two people is characterized by a high frequency of exchanges of <u>opposite</u> kinds of behavior. A symmetrical relationship is one in which the interaction between two people is characterized by a high frequency of <u>the same</u> kinds of behavior.

One may usually identify these relationship styles by observing the exchanges of analogic behavior. For example, in a relationship labeled complementary, one might observe what is often described as a one-up, one-down exchange. For example:

<u>Person One</u>	<u>Person Two</u>
Leans Forward	Leans Back
Commands	Acquiesces
Head Erect	Head Down
Loud Voice	Soft Voice
Do This!	Yes, Dear.

The typical explanation for exchanges like the above is that one person is in a dominant position and the other is in a powerless or submissive position. However, this generally accepted interpretation is not consistent with the systems framework. Rather, from a systems perspective, each person in a relationship is understood to be equally powerful and the old meaning of "control" no longer applies. Thus, one could characterize a complementary relationship as one in which the members are using opposite behavior in an attempt to narrow down the number of possible next moves by the other. Complementary behavior can therefore e construed as unilateral efforts to regulate a relationship, efforts which must fail, since a relationship, by definition, is bilateral (Palazzoli, Boscolo, Cecchin & Prata, 1978). Dominance which seems to "cause" submission may look like "control" from a linear perspective. However, reciprocally, submission which seems to create a momentary stoppage of dominant behavior also can be construed as an attempt to change that behavior. According to Bateson (Brand, 1974), in a relationship the illusion of the possibility of unilateral control is often the problem.

In a relationship labeled symmetrical, one might observe escalating exchanges of the same kinds of behavior. Examples of exchanges characterizing symmetrical relationships are as follows:

Person One	**Person Two**
Commands..	Commands
Shouts..	Shouts
Scowls...	Scowls
Attacks..	Attacks
Do This!...	Do That!

It is important to note at this point that complementary and symmetrical exchanges are good or bad only relative to context. Both seem to be a part of every relationship, including those considered to be well-functioning. However, in truly effective relationships there also seems to be something more. Thus a third relationship style, *parallel*, was defined by Lederer and Jackson (1967), and later refined by Scoresby and Christensen (1976). Research by Harper, Scoresby and Boyce (1977) suggests that the parallel relationship style is of a higher logical order than are complementary or symmetrical relationships, which are comprised of behaviors either logically the same or logically the opposite.

A parallel relationship is one in which each person alternates in the complementary, or one-up/one-down, positions and includes a combination of both symmetrical and complementary behaviors. Further, both members of the relationship are able to accept responsibility for things that go wrong between them. There is a high level and high quality of information exchange with approximately the same ratio of listening and expression on the part of each member. Decisions tend to be made by consensus, with a sharing of information and consideration for the ideas of both.

Parallel relationships are characterized particularly by greater variation of behaviors and are not limited to exchanges of the same (symmetrical) or opposite (complementary) behaviors, although these may be a part of the relationship. Parallel relationships seem divested of the power struggle, with each member willing to reciprocally take the one-down position from time to time based on the merits of the ideas of the other. A greater frequency of logically different behavior, i.e., different from more of the same or opposite behaviors, is observed. People in parallel relationships seem to recognize the inherent bilateral nature of relationships.

Wholeness

From a systems perspective we understand that the whole is greater than the sum of the parts, or $1 + 1 = 3$. Two people relating together are not independent. Rather, they mutually interact with one another. It is their interaction which adds the third element to the above equation, or member 1 + member 2 + the relationship dynamics = 3.

In any relationship, the people involved are mutually responsive to one another. When looking at a family, one must see the organismic whole as well as the way every individual acts in relation to all the others. One must look at the organization of the system, or the structure, which emerges as a function of the interaction of the members of that system. One must understand that only when studied in the context of the whole can the behavior of any one individual be fully understood.

As the number of members of a system increases, the complexity of the system also increases. A dyad is comprised of the two persons plus the relationship between them, or three units. A family of five has five persons plus ten relationships, or fifteen units. Further, each relationship in a system affects every other person and every other relationship to some degree. For as Bowen (1976, p.76) has noted, the triangle may well be, "The smallest stable relationship system." Thus, while a dyad may be relatively stable during calm times, as soon as difficulties arise, a third person is often drawn in to form a triangle, or a two against one situation, in order to solve a problem. Indeed, the concept of wholeness moves our family of five persons into a very complex system comprised of five persons, ten relationships and twenty-seven triangles, for a total of forty-two units!

To summarize, wholes must be understood as being different from the sum of their parts. Further, given the interrelatedness of components, a change in one part will have an impact on the whole. Rather than being independent elements, communication exchanges are inseparable. The total system has a unique coherence and may thus be said to be non-summative. That is, adding the parts together will not produce the whole and members are not independent of one another as in the case with summativity.

That which we choose to call a "heap," the phenomenon in which we do not observe interrelatedness, would be summativity. Change in one element would occur in isolation from other elements since the parts are not connected and thus do not have the property of wholeness. In addition, the total of the elements equals the whole. However, as one begins to think and observe from a systems perspective, one can no longer discern such unrelated phenomena.

It is interesting to note at this point that as one thinks in terms of an interrelatedness of all elements in all systems, the possibility that a "heap" exists is reduced to zero, except for instructional purposes. However, if summativity in any phenomenon is not observed, the property of non-summativity becomes the only property possible and thus self-destructs since its opposite identity member, summativity, has no meaning.

The above discussion illustrates the recurring dilemma which we have encountered as we have attempted to define key concepts within the systems framework. We use the construct summative/non-summative to explain the concept of wholeness. However, as our discussion progresses it became apparent that while useful in one sense, the summative/non-summative construct does not fit the assumption suggested by systems theory of a constantly conjoined universe in which all elements are interrelated.

What we have done is to use a construct from one theory (one in which independent elements are possible) to explain another theory (one in which all elements are assumed to be interrelated). We recognize the dilemma and it only reinforces our awareness of the inadequacies of our language system in explaining interrelated phenomena. We therefore reach into other theories for concepts which may be useful in bridging the gap and yet we realize that this device used for teaching purposes in not entirely satisfactory. We recognize the need for a richer language for describing relational concepts, a language that makes sense and is able to bridge other models and thus facilitate a change in epistemology.

Summary and Conclusion

A dilemma similar to that described in relation to the summativity/non-summativity construct is encountered when dealing with cause or purpose relative to a systems perspective. Systems often are described as purposive, or goal oriented. The organization or structure, the network of relationships, and the nature of the relationships within a system exist relative to the purpose of the system. The interrelationships of parts qualify the joint behavior of members of a system in accordance with the purpose of a system.

However, specifying the purpose or goal of a system is problematic without making recourse to intrapsychic processes such as needs or desires of individual members. This activity is not legitimate in systems theory. And to state that the purpose or goal of a system is to maintain itself begs the question of the assumption of the purpose or goal of a system.

Goals and purposes of systems, therefore, tend to be inferential and definitional like systems themselves. Perhaps that which we call "heaps" or "aggregates" are not systems because, and only because, we have not observed a regularity or interrelationship of parts and a purpose or goal behind the interrelations which might exist but have not been observed. In a sense, it is like calling a weed a weed only because we have not found a practical use for the plant we call a weed.

Observing regularities does not mean that the regularities exist *per se*. Yet, we observe redundant patterns of familial interaction and it becomes useful to define the family as a system. It is also useful for us to describe distinctions between plants and animals. However, given another model, such a distinction may not be useful, and we may find it more meaningful to describe the distinction between living and non-living phenomena.

We are accustomed to thinking of a family as having a mother, father, and children. However, we are now aware of the existence of many viable alternative family forms: single parent, restructured, same-sex, kibbutz, commune, to name but a few. These may all be construed appropriately as family systems, although to many some of these alternatives may be perceived as "weeds."

To say that a system's purpose is to receive inputs, process these inputs, and produce outputs to other systems is another possibility. Indeed, this is what it does. However, in terms of goal or purpose, this too is problematic in its circularity. Therefore, we must recognize that it is we who as observers choose and find it useful to define families, schools, communities, etc., as systems and to infer goals and purposes. At the same time, we must acknowledge that as long as we see ourselves as observers outside the system, we are operating at the level of first-order cybernetics and are not truly consistent with systems theory as understood from the level of second-order cybernetics. Further, it is only at the level of first-order cybernetics that we continue to diagnose, assess and treat families from the position of expert. Thus, while our paradigm may have begun to shift as we moved from thinking about individuals to a consideration of families and the larger context, the revolution in our epistemologies provided by systems theory does not really take place until we can think and operate from the perspective of second-order cybernetics.

Chapter 4

SECOND-ORDER CYBERNETICS: DEFINTION OF CONCEPTS

> [W]e are now in the possession of the truism that a description (of the universe) implies one who describes it (observes it). What we need now is the description of the "describer" or, in other words, we need a theory of the observer.
>
> Heinz von Foerster

The primary distinguishing feature between first-order cybernetics and second-order cybernetics is the position of the observer. From this distinction flow the differences in our understanding of systems theory and related concepts at these two level. At the level of first-order cybernetics, the observer remains outside the system. Thus, the system or context has a connotation of being "out there," an idea that is consistent with Newtonian physics or traditional science, the modernist perspective. At the level of second-order cybernetics, the observer is understood to be part of the system, with no "out there," an idea that is consistent with quantum physics or a postmodernist perspective.

The ramifications of this shift are extremely significant. For example, the possibility of objectivity no longer exists for reality is understood as completely self-referential. That is, as we observe, we influence that which we are attempting to understand. Everything we see is filtered through our personal frame of reference and our very presence changes the context. Therefore, we do not discover behavior, we create it. Stated somewhat differently, the behavior we observe and the meaning we assign to it are our constructions.   In our total interconnectedness, we recognize that we are all involved in each other's destiny and that reality is a co-creation in which everyone participates.

While we continue to focus on patterns, relationships and process, we understand that we are in the system and there is no reference to an outside environment. The emphasis shifts, therefore, to recursion and to an understanding, from within, of the internal structure of systems. This is done through a consideration of the following concepts which we have chosen for inclusion in this chapter:

Autopoiesis

Consensual Domains

Epistemology of Participation

Feedback

Non-Purposeful Drift

Openness and Closedness

Reality as a Multiverse

Structural Coupling

Structural Determinism

Wholeness and Self-Reference

Autopoiesis

The literal meaning of the term autopoiesis is self-generation. As a construct from the perspective of second-order cybernetics, it refers to the processes within various systems, or the ways that the parts relate, that create a particular unity according to which we recognize it as a certain kind of system. For example, in the ongoing process of interacting according to certain recognizable patterns, family members create rules. These rules comprise a boundary by which the family system distinguishes itself and may be distinguished from the larger suprasystem of which it is a part.

The family and the boundary require each other but they do not cause each other. That is, in order to recognize a family system as distinct there must be a boundary. At the same time, in order for the boundary to exist there must be a set of interactions by means of which we may define it as a family system.   Both exist as a function of ongoing recursive processes between family members. Therefore, they are considered to be essential elements of the unitary process described as autopoiesis.

Consensual Domains

Consensual domains are generated as participants structurally couple, or mutually interact and coexist, in the context of a common language system (Maturana & Varela, 1992). In other words, as the participants in a relationship interact with each other, a particular reality is created as a function of their interactions. Relative to the process of observation and the assumption that the observer is part of the observed, we may speak of two orders of consensual domains, or two different kinds of realities.

First-order consensual domains have been defined as those we study. Second-order consensual domains are those of which we are a part. That is, as "observers," we act as though we were external to a situation and "observe" it (first-order) and ourselves (second-order) observing. In the process of these two sets of activities we are simultaneously creating the reality of the consensual domain we are attempting to observe. Once again, recursion, mutuality and circularity not only are assumed but they represent the keys to understanding the construct of consensual domains.

Epistemology of Participation

To speak of an epistemology of participation is to denote the ongoing recursive process in which individuals and systems interact and make adjustments to each other as all evolve and change. It also is to recognize that reality is a co-creation and that it is inappropriate to decide how something should or should not be or what constitutes progress from any one perspective. Finally, it is to acknowledge that ultimately all knowledge is subjective and that in our attempts to understand reality we are saying as much about ourselves as we are about what it is we are seeking to describe.

For the family therapist it is important to become aware that given this perspective, we no longer speak of treating individuals and families. Rather, therapy becomes a process of mutual perturbations and compensations on the part of both therapist and family members. It is a dance in which all are involved and whatever we create, we create it together. Further, it is not appropriate for the therapist to decide how a family should be; the therapist does not act in the role of expert, or social engineer. Everyone is recognized as having his or her own particular expertise and it is the client who decides the goals of therapy. The therapist assumes a role more akin to facilitator as she or he participates with the client in the process of change.

Feedback

While we may speak of positive feedback at the level of second-order cybernetics, it is appropriate to do so only if we see it as complementary to, and therefore a component of, negative feedback at a higher order of recursion. That is, the system is always operating to maintain that system. Or, "The product of an autopoietic system is always itself" (Becvar & Becvar, 1996, p. 78). And since it is autonomous, meaning that it is a self-contained whole and there is no reference to an outside environment, the appearance of change or instability at one level is understood as system-maintenance activity, or stability at another level.

For the therapist it thus becomes essential to consider the larger ecological balance of the system as a whole. For example, how do current behaviors participate in the maintenance of the system? What will be the ramifications for the marriage of change in the wife without the participation of the husband? How much change is too much?

Non-Purposeful Drift

Systems interact with each other in a given context through a process of mutual influence, feedback and adaptation. The range of these interactions is a function of the limits of what is possible given the structure of the systems involved. However, the context within which these systems interact is not itself deterministic. Environment does not determine structure. Rather, structure emerges as a function of reciprocal interactions and the potential for reciprocal interactions is a function of the structure created through earlier reciprocal interactions.

What all of this means is that we cannot speak in terms of cause and effect in a linear fashion. When change occurs, it is a response to a change in context mutually created by both systems. Accordingly, we speak of the life of a system as a process of nonpurposeful drift. And non-purposeful drift continues as long as the system exists.

When working with families, therefore, we recognize that we do not change them. We work in partnership with family members to facilitate the creation of a new context which is supportive of the behaviors desired by the family. What is more, we recognize the limits of what is possible given both structure and context.

Openness and Closedness

As already mentioned, at the level of second-order cybernetics, what we have is organizational closure. The system plus the observer, or therapist, are understood to be mutually interacting within a larger system whose boundary is closed. There is no reference to an outside environment. The idea of inputs into the system from outside is thus replaced by the concept of perturbations from within. And the change process involves the structure of the system, or the way the organization of the whole is maintained.

As the therapist and members of the family system converse, each question or comment and each response simultaneously perturbs and is compensated for by everyone involved. In the course of the conversation a new pattern of relationships may emerge, or the family members may evolve new, hopefully more satisfactory, ways of being a family. The whole is maintained but its internal structure, or the relationships between members, is changed. And all of this occurs within a system considered to be organizationally closed.

Reality as a Multiverse

From the perspective of second-order cybernetics the idea of a universe self-destructs. In its place we speak of a multiverse of individual perceptions. Each of us is understood to live in and create reality in a slightly different manner based on our particular unique combination of heredity, experience, presuppositions, values and beliefs. Each of us thus lives in and creates a slightly different reality. And each person's reality is true and valid for that person.

When a family therapist works with a family of four, for example, what she or he really works with are five families, or the perceptions of that family from the perspective of the four family members as well as of the therapist. And each person's reality must be acknowledged and respected.

You might find an illustration of this idea by comparing notes with one or more of your siblings about how things were in your family when you were children. What you probably will find is that your stories vary, that you see things somewhat differently. Indeed, each of you grew up in a slightly different family based on what was going on when you arrived, who else was present, the age and circumstances of your parents, your and their unique characteristics, etc. Such is the nature of the multiverse.

Structural Coupling

Structural coupling refers to the degree to which systems are able to mutually co-exist. It also refers to the compatibility or congruence between a particular organizational unity, or system, and its environment. For systems survive by fitting with one another and with the other aspects of their context. If the fit is insufficient, the system will die (Maturana & Varela, 1992).

As we think about individuals and families who thrive as compared with those who do not, we get a sense of the degree to which structural coupling has or has not taken place. Those systems which function according to the rules and laws of society, for example, do much better than those who choose to violate these social norms.

Similarly, we can think of structural coupling as having been achieved, or not, by the extent to which we are able to connect with our clients. As we are able to communicate in a manner that is mutually understandable we establish a fit that is compatible and congruent. By analogy, we could say that we are all tuned into and operating on the same wave length. And certainly we may observe the "death" of a relationship in which such a congruence was not achieved.

Structural Determiniam

According to the concept of structural determinism, we recognize that it is the system which determines the range of structural variations which are possible without loss of identity. That is, the system is limited in terms of what it can and cannot do as a function of its particular structure. Further, what a system does is always correct; it is organized to do what it does.

The fact that birds can fly and human beings cannot is a function of their particular structure. Because human beings cannot fly does not mean there is something wrong with them. Rather, they are organized to walk, run, hop, skip and jump and that is what they do. Similarly, families are organized to do what they do and whatever they do is logical given their particular structure. And what they do is only "wrong" from the perspective of an outsider who chose to label what they do wrong. Accordingly, we must understand how behaviors, even those considered undesirable, fit in a given family context. And if change is to occur, the context or structure must shift in order that new behaviors become logical.

Wholeness and Self-Reference

From a perspective that recognizes the observer as part of the observed, we become aware that whatever we see reflects, or says as much about us as it does about the object of our observations. This is the perspective of wholeness, or self-reference, which emphasizes the internal structure of the system and the mutual connectedness between all participants. With autonomy, or organizational closure, we acknowledge that we cannot get outside ourselves and our frames of reference. Thus, absolute objectivity becomes an impossibility and awareness of our inevitable subjectivity is essential.

Summary and Conclusion

From the perspective of second-order cybernetics, we must recognize in our work with various client systems that our story about the client is but one of many possible views. It is also necessary to be aware that how we choose to story our clients will influence what we see and what we do as well as how they will respond to us. What is more, although we may create, based on our story, a set of interventions which happen to be successful, this does not mean that our story described the way the family "really" was. Rather, all that we can say is that it was a useful story and that many others also might have been useful.

We become aware that we are always part of the story. We therefore must also acknowledge that we participate in the creation of problems as well as of solutions. Indeed, failure to recognize this shared responsibility may inadvertently participate in the creation of problems for our clients which are greater than those for which they initially sought our help.

Chapter 5

FAMILY INTERPRETIVE SYSTEMS/STORIES

> What we perceive or overlook in the field of our potential experience depends on the framework or concepts we have in our minds.
>
> Icheiser

As you read this book, you are learning about a model of the world, a story, a map of the reality we assume exists but cannot know in an absolute sense. Systems theory, like other theories, is only one explanation. Systems theory, like other theories, is an invention of people for, "man cannot transcend himself ..., so that no matter what modes of perception or what sorts of world interpretation he chooses, they are still his own" (Seidler, 1979, p.52).

We social scientists often view what we do as unique to us as professionals. Indeed, we seek valid explanations which we can use to understand, predict and control our world. Kelly (1955), however, makes a useful contribution with his description of people in general, as well as scientists, being engaged in the same enterprise. He sees all people as scientists who observe, form hypotheses, and conduct experiments to test the validity of their predictions relative to their interpretive systems. This process takes a circular course according to the frame of reference, or interpretive system, all of us as "scientists" use. Accordingly, we are free to see the world and interpret its events in a manner consistent with our frame of reference. At the same time, we are constrained by our particular perspective from definitions which might be possible in the context of another framework.

Consistent with a postmodern, second-order cybernetics perspective, we may say that ours is a storied reality. From such a perspective, our theories, or stories, are understood as the stuff of human experience, encompassing our sciences, histories, politics, economics, and religions - our personal as well as our professional lives. Thus, every conversation, every theory, may be seen as an exercise in story telling. And we may become aware that the stories we tell ourselves guide our lives and our work and ultimately create our reality. Indeed, our stories may live our lives for us.

To speak of stories rather than "reality" means that "truth" in the tradition of logical positivism is not available to us. According to the notion of a storied reality, the form of our relationships with self, others, creatures and things necessarily takes the form of the way we story ourselves and others. In the words of Howard Mair (1988, p. 127):

> Stories are habitations. We live in and through stories. They conjure worlds. We do not know the world other than story world. Stories inform life. They hold us together and keep us apart. We inhabit the great stories of our culture. We live through stories. We are lived by the stories of our race and place. It is this enveloping and constituting function of stories that is especially important to sense more fully. We are, each of us, locations where the stories of our place and time become partially tellable.

The truth or falseness of an interpretive system, or story, is not discernable. However, the degree of usefulness of a story is personally decidable relative to context. In general, we probably will choose to use the theory or frame of reference that seems better than its rivals.

And "better" means when it can explain and predict the facts and solve the problems of interest to us.

Both individual members of families and family units have interpretive systems and stories to which they make recourse. Spouses bring to their new family the elements of the interpretive systems they learned in their families of origin. This merger of stories in the married couple is characterized by a process of taking parts of each and creating a new frame which fits for their unique relationship. Indeed, it has been suggested that people are, at least in part, attracted to each other on the basis of the compatibility of their interpretive systems.

To the degree that there is agreement or disagreement of frames of reference, we could assume a compatibility or lack of harmony plus pressure on one another to adapt and/or modify their behavior and thus their stories. However, according to Kuhn (1970), an interpretive system can never be entirely adequate. There are some things it cannot explain or predict and there will always be at least one "violation of paradigm expectation." Such variations are called anomalies.

Anomalies are initially unnoticed. An interpretive system implicitly defines and imposes boundaries which prevent the early recognition of anomalies, which are thus unimportant or irrelevant at the outset. Sooner or later, however, these anomalies are recognized for what they are, e.g., genuine problems for the paradigm, or interpretive system. Attempts may be made to assimilate an anomaly within the interpretive frame or to adapt the theory or story to account for the anomaly, thereby eliminating the apparent conflict. If an anomaly cannot be assimilated by a theory, the model itself is threatened. Indeed, the inability of an existing theory to handle such an anomaly usually signals the beginning of a search for a new theory (Kuhn, 1970).

If the anomalous phenomenon is sufficiently deviant, scientists may turn their attention from existing research to an investigation of and explanation for this phenomenon. Such efforts may involve a questioning of the adequacy of the standard paradigm and may result in the formulation of a new paradigm, or theory, in which the phenomenon fits and is thus no longer an anomaly. And so the process of scientific "revolutions" repeats itself.

Kuhn's model of scientific revolutions is a useful metaphor to explain the "progress of science" within families. As stated previously, one could describe the initial formation of a new family, at least in part, as an apparent compatibility and merging of interpretive frames. An interpretive frame can be thought of as containing within it a set of constructs of paired opposites which provide the basis for experiencing meaning for events that occur in the perceptual field. A few of the constructs which may exist within such an interpretive frame may include the following:

Category	Opposite Category
Good	Bad
Cooperative	Competitive
Easy	Hard
Strong	Weak
Support	Neglect
Happy	Sad
Passive	Active

A given stimulus event may activate certain of these paired opposites in order to provide a meaning for the experience. For example, the stimulus event "religion" may activate any of the following:

Category	Opposite Category
Good	Bad
Strong	Weak
Support	Neglect
Happy	Sad

The constructs in an interpretive system provide direct links to experienced meaning, feelings, and action. The bi-polar nature of the constructs parallels a positive or negative affective response. People would therefore describe a religious experience according to their interpretive systems and behave in a manner that is logical to it. This process can be illustrated as follows:

It is likely that each newly married couple will experience anomalies in the behavior of the other which do not fit the interpretive system brought with them from their families of origin. These frames of reference were familized into them in their years of experience within their families. Each individual may seek to impose his/her set of constructs on the marital relationship.

Daily contact provides a number of issues and experiences for the discovery of anomalies in the behavior of the other in such areas as sex, degree of separateness acceptable, nurturance, money management, parenting practices, etc. Successful marriages and families develop a new interpretive system unique to the new family. They retain commonly shared constructs from their families or origin, but evolve new interpretive systems, new stories, when anomalies are experienced.

The members of a couple may experience a minimum of difficulty in adjusting and forming a new family if their interpretive systems are flexible rather than rigid. An interpretive system with the meta-perspective that there is more than one interpretation can transcend any specific explanation and look for alternatives when anomalies are encountered around specific issues. This is important for the initial adjustment to marriage as well as for dealing with subsequent developmental crises which occur throughout the family life cycle.

A couple may be aware of certain explicit rules brought from the stories of their families or origin. However, the rules that are the most important are probably implicit. Such rules are tied to corresponding interpretive systems and may not be consciously experienced. Rather, they are generally activated automatically. These are the implicit "should," or the "way it is supposed to be," for each role in the family, e.g., husband, wife, mother, father, breadwinner, keeper of the castle.

A family's interpretive system, or set of stories, also may be inferred from the metaphors it's members use to describe themselves. The types and kinds of labels assigned reveal how a family defines reality as well as the categories which comprise its interpretive system. Such metaphors are basic to the understanding of each family's story.

Within a family, the rules, values, and beliefs in the interpretive system must be flexible if the family is to contribute to the normal development of its members. There needs to be both stability and change. A couple may change its ideas about marriage and family from what they anticipated to what is actually experienced. Similarly, the interpretive system necessary while children are young must change when children become adolescents if the family is to continue to be happy and to foster normal development. Family problems may lie in the failure of the family to make necessary transitions to different stages during the course of the development of its members. A functional interpretive system is subscribed to with a certain tentativeness and is sufficiently flexible to allow for movement to successive stages of growth and development.

It is our position that a family's interpretive system is most useful to its members when it is based on a systems perspective, i.e., a frame that sees the interdependence of the members of a family system. Further, we believe that the useful interpretive system would contain knowledge of normal developmental stages of individuals and families and would thus allow for a smooth transition from one stage to another. It is also useful, as mentioned above, for the interpretive system to contain a meta-perspective which allows for the possibility of alternative explanations or new metaphors, and contains rules for changing the rules about the family and family life as the need arises. This system is open and yet closed, and can help family members acquire what seems to be a necessary balance between the seemingly contradictory but essential ingredients of a satisfying relationship. The family provides a context that defines stability relative to its ability to change.

In any relationship there will be "violations of the paradigm," or deviations which are anomalies only from a specific interpretive system. With relativistic thinking, there is a greater probability that these anomalies can be given a constructive definition rather than that they will contribute to the deterioration of the relationship. A reframe or new interpretation thus becomes possible, and with it, different feelings and different action alternatives.

Family therapy approaches consistent with the notion that ours is a storied reality often focus on the stories, or narratives (White & Epston, 1990), which guide clients' lives. The therapist engages with clients in a process of reauthoring their lives. According to Howard (1991, p. 194), such an approach may be summarized as follows:

Life - The Stories We Live By;
Psychopathology - Stories Gone Mad;
Psychotherapy - Exercises in Story Repair.

Chapter 6

FAMILY DEVELOPMENT THROUGH THE LIFE CYCLE

...the developmental conceptual framework...brings together from rural sociologists the idea of stages of the life cycle, from child psychologists and human development researchers concepts of developmental needs and tasks, from the sociology of the professions the idea of a family as a set of mutually contingent careers, and from the structure function and interaction theorists such concepts as age and sex roles, plurality patterns, functional prerequisites, and other concepts which view the family as a system of interacting actors.

Rueben Hill and Roy H. Rodgers

Viewing the family as a system requires that we look at the dynamic interaction of individual members as well as at the relationship between the members as well as the family and other systems. We understand that relationships are characterized by rules or redundant patterns. We find that individuals and families may arrive at very similar situations even though they may have started out in many different ways. We recognize that the redundant patterns form boundaries which distinguish systems from one another. And we realize that a balance between stability and change is necessary for the attainment of a well functioning family.

We might say that the family maintains stability through change that may occur relative to the needs of individual members and of the system as a whole. Thus we juxtapose flexibility and predictability, with each the context for the other, within the concept of system. A framework for understanding this balance is provided by various theories of individual and family development.

Indeed, knowledge of developmental stages is useful in order both to facilitate appropriate action when necessary and to avoid overreacting when little or no action is required (Watzlawick, Weakland & Fisch, 1974). A well-functioning family evolves relative to both external and internal pressures. It has an interpretive system which is sufficiently informed so that change at the appropriate time in appropriate amounts is anticipated and accommodated. In other words, there are rules for changing the rules.

By contrast, according to Haley (1973), it is at the point at which change relative to developmental issues is called for that families often get stuck. For example, a family may come into therapy for help with a child who is having problems in school. The therapist would do well to consider the ages of the parents and the child as well as the position of the child in the family. Therapy is likely to be more productive if attention is paid to such developmental issues as the need for a change in the rules as young children move into adolescence. Similarly, awareness that the struggle around mid-life career issues may be impacting the ability of the couple to parent effectively may influence the course of therapy.

Individuals as well as families may be conceptualized as proceeding through developmental cycles in which different stages are characterized by different sources of conflict and solidarity. Further, cycles of growth may be understood as occurring simultaneously relative to physical, emotional, cognitive and relational development. However, although there is a wide variety of theoretical frameworks dealing with such patterns of growth and development, we will discuss only two of the many we have found to be useful.

The key to Erik Erikson's (1963) eight stage theory of individual development and the life cycle lies in the concept of the attainment of "inner sameness and continuity" by a progression through developmental stages. Each of these stages has specific tasks with which the individual must deal, with each stage building upon the one that preceded it. According to Erikson, "psychosocial development proceeds by critical stages - 'critical' being a characteristic of turning points, of moments of decision between progress and regression, integration and retardation" (1963, pp. 270-271). The individual thus is seen as a creative being who is faced with particular challenges at particular points in life, and society is viewed as responding to maintain the proper progression for this "succession of potentialities." The following chart presents Erikson's eight stages and the developmental tasks appropriate to each according to his framework:

ERIK ERIKSON'S "EIGHT AGES OF MAN"

STAGE	DEVELOPMENTAL TASK
I. Oral -Sensory	Basic Trust vs. Mistrust
II. Muscular-Anal	Autonomy vs. Shame & Doubt
III. Locomotor-Genital	Initiative vs. Guilt
VI. Latency	Industry vs. Inferiority
V. Puberty & Adolescence	Identity vs. Role Confusion
VI. Young Adulthood	Intimacy vs. Isolation
VII. Adulthood	Generativity vs. Stagnation
VIII. Maturity	Ego Integrity vs. Despair

This framework describes stages of individual development. Viewed systemically, the family is the context in which these developmental tasks are or not mastered. A well-functioning family provides a context in which each member masters appropriate developmental tasks and is thus prepared to interface successfully with other systems. At the same time, we can also describe a stage critical family life cycle schema which broadens our understanding of the family system at any given point in time. A summary of such a model is presented by means of the following chart:

*STAGES OF THE FAMILY LIFE CYCLE

STAGE	EMOTION ISSUES	STAGE CRITICAL TASKS
1. Unattached Adult	Accepting Parent-Offspring	a. Differentiation from Family of Origin b. Development of Peer Relations c. Initiation of Career
2. Newly Married Couple	Commitment to the Marriage	a Formation of Marital System b. Making Room for Spouse with Family and Friends
3. Childbearing	Accepting New Members into the System	a. Adjusting Marriage to Make Room b. Taking on Parenting Roles c. Making Room for Grandparents
4. Preschool-Age	Accepting the New Personality	a. Adjusting Family to Needs of Each Child b. Coping with Energy Drain and Lack of Privacy
5. School-Age Child	Allowing Child to Establish Relationships Outside the Family	a. Extending Family Interactions with Society b. Encouraging Educational Achievement

(*From Barnhill & Longo, 1978; Carter & McGoldrick, 1980: Duvall, 1962)

STAGE	EMOTION ISSUES	STAGE CRITICAL TASKS
6. Teenage Child	Increasing Flexibility of Family Boundaries to Allow Child's Independence	a. Shifting Parent-Child Relationship to Balance Freedom and Limits b. Refocusing on Mid-Life Career and Marital Issues
7. Launching Center	Accepting Exits from and Entries into the Family	a. Releasing Young Adult Children into Work, College, Marriage b. Maintaining a Supportive Home Base
8. Middle-Age Parents	Letting go and Facing Each Other Again	a. Rebuilding Marriage b. Realigning Family to Include Spouses of Children and Grandchildren c. Dealing with Aging of Older Generation
9. Retirement	Accepting Retirement	a. Adjusting to Retirement/Old Age b. Coping with Death of Parents and Spouse c. Closing or Adapting Family Home d. Maintaining Couple and Individual functioning e. Supporting Middle Generation

By using the two conceptualizations just outlined in combination, we are able to understand the individual in terms of the process of growth and development, to see him or her in the context of his or her family at any given point in its developmental process, and to anticipate the normal kinds of issues with which families in general may be faced as all grow and evolve. To illustrate this idea, we will now take a brief look at the life cycle of a hypothetical family, considering the processes of system formation and evolution over time. Although we will not dwell on problem formation or resolution, we will attempt to describe the kinds of intertwining issues and troublesome transition points at which families may easily get stuck. Although not the case with this family, as mentioned earlier, it is at such points that we often see families in therapy. Hence the necessity for understanding the complexity of family growth and development.

As you will recall from our chart, Stage 1 in the family life cycle focuses on the unattached adult. The emotion issues center around the acceptance of parent-offspring separation as the young adult seeks to establish his or her life. The stage critical tasks include differentiation from family of origin, the development of peer relations and the initiation of a career. From Erikson's framework we also have the issue of intimacy vs. isolation. It is this context that we first encounter the relationship system of Carol and Ted, aged 25 and 27 respectively.

Having taken the first steps in the process of separating from their families of origin, both are involved with beginning careers and with the formation of a stable and meaningful relationship with one another. Although not married, Carol and Ted live together. Carol has a degree in elementary education and teaches third grade in a neighboring district. Ted is in graduate school, completing his MBA, and he works part time as a check-out clerk at a nearby grocery store.

After college Carol had shared an apartment with two other girls. Ted lived at home during his undergraduate years but took an apartment nearer the campus when he began graduate school. During his final year of study, the couple decided that living separately no longer made sense. This was a time of adjustment as Carol and Ted were now interacting on a daily basis and were struggling to harmonize the relationship rules which each had brought from his or her family of origin. And although they lived in an environment that was accepting of their life style, the messages received and processed from their respective families were not as favorable.

Carol's parents had a particularly difficult time accepting and understanding how to relate to Ted and their daughter in the context of this living arrangement. They saw a deviation from the family rules and gave feedback aimed at returning the system to its previous state. While not as upset, Ted's parents would have preferred that the couple wait until they were married before sharing living quarters. Thus the families of origin were a part of the relationship system of Carol and Ted.

The couple is now in the process of evolving a comfortable and acceptable pattern of interaction for their relationship within the context of factors such as those described above. And having decided that they wish to make a permanent commitment to one another, they plan to marry as soon as Ted completes graduate school and finds a job.

When next we encounter Carol and Ted it is as a newly married couple who are dealing with the Stage 2 emotion issue of commitment to the marriage. Their critical tasks for this phase of the family life cycle include formation of the marital system and adjusting their relationships with family and friends to accommodate the presence of a spouse. They have resolved the developmental task of young adulthood to some extent by making the choice of marriage. The extent to which they successfully complete this task will be reflected in the degree of intimacy they are able to achieve in their marital relationship.

Although the couple had expected little or no difference in their relationship, they soon find that marriage is a very different context and the transition proves to be somewhat stressful. Each has new expectations of the other brought from their families of origin. As a married couple they experience and are experienced differently in their social environment, which gradually expands and becomes a context for new pressures as there are greater inputs of information into the system. And with the legalization of their relationship they find themselves more involved with their in-laws as each maintains a role within his or her respective family of origin.

Carol and Ted have agreed that both will work for at least three more years before starting a family. They continue to be involved in establishing their careers. They are able to put away some money for the future and still have sufficient income to live comfortably. The rules of their relationship provide time to be both together and apart, either with friends or alone. In time they work out a relationship of mutual support so that they can complete routine tasks and still have time to play together.

The couple enjoys going camping and hiking, and summer vacations are sometimes spent backpacking or mountain climbing. During the week both are busy with their jobs but each finds the other interesting to talk to and be with during their times alone.   They evolve a circle of friends that they are comfortable visiting with from time to time and they keep in touch with their families at least once a week. All in all, a fairly stable pattern.

As they near the end of the second year of marriage, Carol and Ted begin to receive increased numbers of messages from both sets of parents about the importance of grandchildren and about how they shouldn't wait too long before becoming parents.   Although they consider the possibility of changing their plans, they ultimately agree to wait and it isn't until about a year and a half later that they decide to have their first child.

However, Carol does not become pregnant immediately and decides to continue working.   Meanwhile, Ted begins to rise in the business world, and with increases in both their salaries they decide to buy a home of their own.   They find it difficult to reconcile their different tastes in picking and furnishing a house, but eventually are able to reach acceptable compromises.   All of these events represent developmental crises, or challenges, and as such are potential sources of problems.   But Carol and Ted have sufficient flexibility to evolve new rules for their relationship as needed and we soon find them moving into the next stage of the family life cycle.

Stage 3 is the childbearing stage and the emotion issue is that of accepting new members into the system.   Adjusting the marriage to make room for children, taking on parenting roles, and making room for grandparents comprise the stage critical tasks.   The individual development stage is that of adulthood and the task that of generativity vs. stagnation both in terms of procreation, and creativity in one's chosen field of endeavor.

Carol and Ted had not been in their new home a year before their first child was born.   Although each is very excited about their baby daughter, Ann, they have some misgivings about their ability to be good parents and are daily becoming more aware of the increased complexity of their little family.   Carol is concerned about whether or not to become a full-time mother and therefore decides to take a maternity leave rather than quitting her job entirely. Ted is not happy with this decision and it is the subject of many heated discussions.

Ted is also resentful of the amount of time which Carol must devote to the baby and he begins to stay out late a couple of nights a week. Carol is tired from all her new activities and becomes upset by what she feels is Ted's lack of interest in the baby. And both must figure out how to handle diplomatically the well-meaning but often intrusive behaviors of the new grandparents.

Eventually Carol and Ted are able to work out a new set of rules for their relationship which gives them time to be a couple as well as parents. Carol decides to resign her teaching position and be a full-time mother. Two years later they have a second child, another daughter, whom they name Ellen. Having successfully weathered the crises of parenthood which accompanied the birth of Ann, they are better able to handle the increasing complexity of their four member family system.

As the children grow into toddlers we now encounter the family in Stage 4 of the family life cycle. With preschool-age children they must accept the new personality of each of their offspring. The family's tasks include adjusting the system to the needs of the children and coping with the energy drain and lack of privacy as a married couple which comes with being parents. Individually, the children must deal first with the developmental tasks of basic trust vs. mistrust followed by autonomy vs. shame and doubt and the family must provide a context for the successful resolution of these tasks. As adults Ted and Carol continue to be concerned with the issue of generativity vs. stagnation.

Carol now begins to evolve a new network of relationships as she becomes better acquainted with the other parents of young children living in their neighborhood. And as she learns to structure and schedule daily routines for herself and the children, she finds time to become involved in local politics and begins taking piano lessons, the fulfillment of some long time dreams. Ted continues to be very occupied with his job, which he finds stimulating and challenging. However, he also spends time with his wife and daughters as he is able, for family time is a high priority.

Although their worlds are very different now, Carol and Ted feel that their relationship is quite satisfactory. They are proud of their little family despite some ups and downs which they consider to be

fairly normal.   And as the need for change emerges, they have
sufficient flexibility to be able to respond appropriately.

The family moves to Stage 5 as first Ann and then Ellen go off to
school. With school-age children, the emotion issue involves allowing
each child to establish relationships outside the family.   The stage
critical tasks revolve around extending the family system to interact
with society and encouraging each child's educational achievement.
Generativity vs. stagnation continue to be developmental concerns of
our adult parents, while for the children, industry vs. inferiority is the
task at hand.

The children move into school with little difficulty and Carol, who
is at first saddened by Ellen's eagerness to go off with her sister each
morning, begins to enjoy the extra time for herself. Afternoons after
school become exciting times as the girls describe their day's activity
for their mother. It is then homework time and Ann and Ellen work at
the kitchen table. Carol usually sits with them, reading a book or
giving some assistance when it is needed.

Both Carol and Ted are interested in their children's educational
activity. They join the parent-teachers association and go together to
parent conferences whenever possible.   When difficulties arise in
school they feel fortunate that they are familiar with the various
teachers and school routines.

As the children make new friends and become more involved in
outside activities, Carol faces a crisis in terms of role adjustment. She
no longer feels totally satisfied staying at home all day. She therefore
begins to think about returning to work, believing that the family
could probably manage if household activities were well planned.

Thus when Ann and Ellen enter the sixth and fourth grades
respectively, Carol returns to teaching third grade, this time in the
same school that her children attend.   The three of them go back and
forth to school together, so child-care is not a problem.   However,
Carol now has much less time at home and it becomes necessary to
make some adjustments in job assignments.

Carol and Ted take turns preparing dinner and doing other major
household chores such as laundry, cleaning and yard work. The girls
are given jobs appropriate to their ages and everyone is expected to
pitch in as needed. Needless to say, this reorganization does not occur
without a certain amount of interpersonal tension and upset.
Gradually, however, the family is able to establish a routine which
includes not only work but also time for play both together and

separately. And Carol and Ted make time to enjoy each other without the children on a regular basis.

We next find the family in Stage 6 as Ann and Ellen reach adolescence. With teenage children, the family emotion issue is that of increasing the flexibility of the family boundaries in order to provide a context in which Ann and Ellen can make more decisions for themselves and thus be more independent. The stage critical tasks include shifting the parent-child relationship to balance freedom and limits, refocusing on mid-life career and marital issues and beginning concerns for the older generation. For the adolescent, identity vs. role confusion is the major issue. For the parents of adolescents it is a time of assessment in terms of how far one has come and how far it is still possible to go in one's life and career.

Ann and Ellen are on their own now as each attends different schools. With Ann in high school, Ellen in junior high school and Carol teaching at the elementary level, everyone is on a different schedule. Carol and Ted find themselves having to change the rules for the girls in response to normal developmental pressures. At the same time, Ann and Ellen are recognizing their limits as well as the increase in responsibility that comes with an increase in "freedom."

Meanwhile, Ted has begun to question his job and to struggle with doubts about the kind of success he can reasonably expect in his chosen career. He considers the possibility of taking several different positions, occasionally going out on job interviews. He spends a great deal of time alone and begins to feel as though he is losing contact with his family. Although Carol and the children try to be understanding of his struggle, each is also involved with her own issues.

Another crisis occurs around Carol's parents. While Ted's parents are handling retirement well, Carol's mother and father are both in ill health and Carol is attempting to help care for them as well as work and be available for her husband and children. She tries to be supportive of Ted, but realizes that she is not as effective as she would like to be. She also longs for more support from Ted with her own burdens.

We will leave the family at this point, returning somewhat later to find them in Stage 7. This stage is termed the launching center and the emotion issue is that of accepting exists from and entries into the family. The tasks involve releasing young adult children into work, college, marriage, etc., while at the same time maintaining a supportive home base. Individually, each family member is in the later phases of the developmental tasks encountered in Stage 6 of the family life cycle.

Carol and Ted find it hard to believe that so many years have passed as they take Ann to college for the first time. It is a happy-sad time, for they are aware that their older daughter is essentially leaving home for good and will no longer be their little girl. Ellen finds it fun to be an "only child," but often rebels at having to take over some of Ann's jobs around the house. Once again, routines must be adjusted, but eventually life becomes a little less hectic with only three different schedules to coordinate.

Carol and Ted begin to spend more time together and are able to support one another when Carol's parents die, Ted's parents move to a retirement community and they have to close up the family homes. Meanwhile, Ted has decided to make a lateral move within his company to a more interesting position. And in an effort to take care of his own needs, he goes fishing on the weekend whenever he can.

Occasionally the couple goes camping as they did when they were younger and they use the time to talk, sometimes about the possibility of Carol's going to graduate school. Carol has decided that she would like to become a school counselor and plans to begin work on a master's degree sometime in the future. She decides to wait until both girls are well into college and the family can more easily afford the cost of another tuition.

Once both girls are in college, Carol and Ted find they enjoy both their increased solitude as well as the occasional noise and confusion which reign when Ann and Ellen come home for vacations, often bringing friends with them. The family also has some difficulties in blending life styles inasmuch as Ann and Ellen have become accustomed to living according to different sets of rules.

When Ann graduates from college, she moves to another city where she has found a job working on a newspaper. She visits her parents occasionally and is often in touch by phone. She is happy with her new life and quickly develops a new circle of friends.

Carol now begins graduate school on a part-time basis while continuing to work. She and Ellen, a junior in college, often compare notes on student life. Ted is pleased with Carol's choice but misses the time they had had to do things together. Carol has to spend many hours attending class and studying. Ted tries to pitch in with more of the housework, but he looks forward to the day when Carol will return to a more predictable routine.

Ted has recently received a promotion which brought with it both a higher salary and the necessity to do some traveling. He would like Carol to be able to go with him on some of these trips. Carol, however, is very involved in her graduate work as well as the demands of her job and doesn't feel free to go with Ted.

When Ellen graduates from college and moves into town, Carol quits her teaching job and goes to school on a full-time basis. Within a year she is able to complete her master's degree in counseling. At the same time, Ann has decided to marry and the family finds itself in the middle of wedding preparations as well as in the process of moving into the next stage of their family life cycle.

Stage 8 is the stage of middle-age parents who must let go of their children and face each other again. Their tasks are to rebuild their marriage as a two person system, to realign their family to include spouses of children and grandchildren and to continue to deal with their own aging parents. Their children are now young adults making choices around intimacy vs. isolation, and as they enter the individual stage of maturity, Ted and Carol will need to deal with the task of ego integrity vs. despair.

Carol and Ted are fond of their son-in-law and they look forward to the day when they will become grandparents. However, remembering their own experience, they do not talk to Ann and her new husband about this subject. They find it an interesting challenge to readjust their thinking about their children now that they are adults. Ellen is enjoying success as a public relations consultant and is intent on pursuing a career, a decision about which her parents have some mixed emotions.

Having returned to the status of married couple without dependent children, Carol and Ted are in the process of renewing their relationship. Carol has taken a part-time job which gives her some flexibility to travel with Ted. They enjoy having Ann and her husband for dinner once in a while most of their contact with Ellen is by phone.

During this period, Ted's father dies and the family decides that Ted's mother will come and live with them. Although everyone is in favor of this choice, it require some adjustment to have another person living in the house. However, Ted's mother is able to help out with household chores, which enhances her sense of usefulness, and Carol appreciates the assistance. They all manage to give each other enough space so that their interactions generally tend to be harmonious.

We come now to the final stage in the family life cycle. Retirement characterizes Stage 9, and accepting retirement and old age is its emotion issue. Adjusting to retirement, coping with the death of parents and/or spouse, closing or adapting the family house, providing support for a more central role of the middle generation, and maintaining their functioning as individuals and as a couple comprise the stage critical tasks for Carol and Ted. This latter task relates to the final resolution of the issue of ego integrity vs. despair with which each began to deal in the previous stage. For their children, the developmental tasks revolve around intimacy vs. isolation and generativity vs. stagnation. And Ann and Ellen are both also interacting in terms of the appropriate stage of their own family life cycles.

Ted decides to retire early, and not long afterward his mother dies. He and Carol now are concerned with the question of how they will spend their remaining years together. Ted would like to sell their house and move to a warmer climate, but Carol prefers to continue working for a few more years and is not anxious to move away from her children.

Carol and Ted agree that they will remain where they are for the time being and Ted finds part-time work as a consultant. He is soon busy again meeting a new series of challenges and finds the people with whom he is working interesting and enjoyable. He and Carol also begin to take weekend trips to the mountains they have always enjoyed climbing. And they continue the process of evolving family rules in response to information from within and without their relationship system as they complete their journey through the family life cycle.

As we have attempted to illustrate with the foregoing, each of the new events within the life cycle, both individual and family, requires a modification of roles and of the rules of the relationships among family members. Indeed, if an event occurs without the appropriate modification in response to that event, a crisis may result. In systemic terms, at least at the level of first-order cybernetics, we would say that the negative feedback loops will tend to escalate in ever more dysfunctional patterns. The system would therefore be moving toward greater chaos, or entropy, as it failed to incorporate new information in a manner consistent with movement toward greater complexity and flexibility, or negative entropy.

Similarly, inappropriate action taken to modify the structure which is otherwise evolving normally may precipitate a crisis within the family. For example, the adolescent needs of Ann and Ellen for greater freedom were normal and to be expected. However, if Carol and Ted had looked upon the expression of these needs as "teenage rebellion" and responded accordingly, the family would in all likelihood have found itself locked in conflict. On the other hand, since the family anticipated such needs by offering opportunities for the exercise of greater freedom on the part of their adolescents, many problems were avoided and the system provided a context which fostered both individual and family development.

Another way of considering the impact of developmental stages within and upon families is to view them from the perspective of the way in which freedom is managed in a family. According to Bender (1976), stringent restrictions of the very young child gradually give way to almost complete freedom at the time when the young adult is ready to leave home. A rather authoritarian mode of behavior on the part of the parent may therefore be functional when children are quite small. However, this mode needs to be revised with the increase in intellectual and moral development of the child. Thus, "Sit down!" to a four year old may become, "You seem quite restless and impatient," to a fifteen year old. Ideally commands are replaced by reason and persuasion, or meta-communication, as the individual matures.

While the family and its members move through their respective life cycles, it is necessary to anticipate an increase in individuation and variation as members interface with more and more diverse systems. A family needs continually to reorganize in the process of maintaining itself, and must increase in complexity to allow for change without self-destruction. Ever increasing amounts of information must be processed by the system. The boundaries must be open to inputs from a variety of new and different systems and yet must be sufficiently defined so that family identity is preserved. Paradoxically, family cohesion is probably best achieved by allowing individuality and variation commensurate to the developmental stages of individual members and thus of the family as a whole.

In addition to normal developmental patterns, unexpected events may also challenge the family and necessitate appropriate action either to modify the structure or to maintain the status quo. For example, the death of a family member must be considered not only relative to the loss of that person but also in terms of its effect on the relationships and the role structure in the family. As pointed out by Bossard (1945), an arithmetic increase or decrease in the number of members in a primary group is accompanied by a corresponding geometric increase or decrease in the number of relationships in that group. The death or loss of one member in a family of five would therefore mean a reduction in the number of relationships from ten to six.

Adaptation of family structure is also necessary when a gradually deteriorating marriage ends in divorce. The family must regroup itself by assuming roles and rules for relationships which are consistent with the change in the system. When the children are living with one parent, they and the other parent will need to relate to each other in a manner different from when the family was living together. The parent with custody will need to institute new rules in order to achieve and maintain stability in the newly constituted family. And the divorced parents will need to evolve a set of rules appropriate for their new relationship, for example, that of co-parents.

Likewise, events such as serious illness of a family member, unemployment of a significant breadwinner, sudden acquisition of wealth or an encounter with the courts all require responses to either modify or maintain the structure according to the new demands upon the system. Further, since it is at the points of transition that families are most susceptible to problem formation, it is important to be aware of the number of stress-producing events impinging upon the system at any given time and to recognize that the capacity of the family to cope well will be affected accordingly.

Certainly we must also consider the family in the context of society. Over the course of history the family has received a great deal of bad press and has been much discussed, often in despairing terms, in recent years. However, we believe that the fact that the family has been able to adapt and persist, both in more traditional forms and in the so-called variant forms, and thus has succeeded in responding to a variety of changes within the suprasystem while still remaining a highly viable entity, is a measure of its great strength.

Far from being "broken down," the family has become a complex system of systems with many different forms. Boundaries have been expanded, new rules for family life have been tested and in some cases have been at least tentatively accepted. Indeed, the family has become much more highly evolved as it interacts with other systems in an increasingly more complex society.

We therefore also believe that the most threatening posture to assume is one that defines the family as being in trouble or as having a problem. For just as is the case in any system that it is often the behavior around a so-called problem which is the problem, so it may be our attitude and behavior toward the family that is problematic. To see only problems may be to participate in maintaining the very situation we have labeled as problematic.

There has indeed been a great increase in the rate of divorce in our society, and the last several decades have been a period of enormous change for both individuals and families. Many have turned elsewhere, possibly in an attempt to find something that was missing in their families. But while divorce, separation, and the loss of a parent are most commonly experienced negatively, in reality the consequences of such events usually result in reorganization rather than breakdown. The family still remains a family, albeit one without a father or a mother, or one with a different form. And if one looks at the experimentation, rebellion and challenges to traditional norms and values as being part of a normal developmental process of family systems, the existence of these behaviors may be seen in a new, less threatening light.

The family is uniquely suited for providing a legitimate context for intimacy and for passing on society's values to succeeding generations. And rather than assuming that the family is in a process of entropy, perhaps it would be more useful for us to recognize its strengths as well as its weaknesses as it struggles for a new identity in a time of great transitions. And we prefer to attempt to understand the logic of all behavior, including that of families, as making sense in context.

Accordingly, we might do well to consider the increasingly complex set of values which characterize our society and thus recognize the increase in new information which the family must process in its daily interactions. We might benefit by understanding the evolution of this system as it moves toward greater complexity consistent with its environment. And we might also conceptualize the family as being in an adolescent stage of development, not unlike to society of which it is a part (Bender, 1976). Such an approach might then lead not only to an awareness of the family's limitations but also to respect for it vigor and potential. One might then argue that in time this "rebellious youth" will in all likelihood mature into an even more responsible "adult," capable of making ever greater contributions to the societal system of which it is a part

We would suggest that one way of interacting effectively with this formidable adolescent might be to give the family greater attention from a developmental rather than from a therapeutic perspective. What is more, as we shift to the level of second-order cybernetics and operate from a postmodern perspective, we are called upon to refrain from deciding how a family should be and support the goals that each family has for itself. Thus, frameworks such as those described in this chapter are understood as offering useful information. However, it is understood that they do not describe the truth and that there is no individual or family that will exactly fit either model. Keeping such provisos in mind relative to all of our theories may enable us as family therapists to be a part of the solution rather than of the problem.

Chapter 7

THE FAMILY AS SYSTEM

Systems theory has evolved in response to plural and often mutually exclusive interpretations of the world, and has spent most of its energies on making an important point, namely that here is another, perhaps more integrated way of looking at things.

Michael Seidler

The family, however defined or structured, is a human *system* consisting of the interactions among its members. While the traditional idea of family refers to father, mother and children, we believe that a family can also be more broadly construed as being whatever one experiences it as being. As family therapists we must recognize that families come in many types and varieties. And while structures may vary and in their variance have different challenges and needs, nevertheless we may attempt to understand them using the same focus on process and pattern that is fundamental to a systems perspective.

Similarly, couples may be married or unmarried, same sex or opposite sex. One hypothesis about the marital dyad, which may also apply to unmarried couples, is that its members are attracted to each other on the basis of the perceived compatibility of the *rules* each brings from his or her family of origin. Portions of these rule systems are combined as part of the process of maintaining the new system in a balance between stability and change. The rules within a family may be thought of as being on a continuum from explicit, or closer to the awareness of family members, to implicit, or outside the awareness of family members but able to be inferred from its redundant patterns.

Observations of a family in action reveal repetitive interaction patterns among family members. These patterns can be construed as unspoken agreements which define various relationships in the family. They characterize and circumscribe The manner in which family members communicate with each other, the nature of the relationships between family members, and how decisions are made in the family. These rules comprise the *boundary* of the family and form a stable, predictable system which is resistant to change. Rule systems tend to be passed on from one generation to the next with only slight modifications.

The boundary of the family system also refers to the discrimination which family members make between "ours" and events out there, e.g., other families, other people other things. The boundary of the family is less distinct in its formation stages and becomes progressively clearer as the family matures. Even in maturity, however, a family's boundary may be modified to include more or less of the family's surroundings, although the rules for inclusion or exclusion remain relatively stable.

The *subsystems* of the family system include its members and the relationships which exist between and among family members. Family members have perceptions, cognitions, affections, and behaviors of which each is aware as belonging to "family." The family system refers to interpersonal processes, and these processes are assumed to be somewhat predictable, providing security and structure for its members. As such, they also fall within the domain of scientific inquiry and understanding.

The family is a separate subsystem of a larger *suprasystem*. It accepts inputs form without (exteroceptive) as well as from within (interoceptive). These inputs are processed and the system emits behaviors as outputs. The inputs within the family are the communication patterns which define each relationship within the family as distinct from every other relationship, and each individual as distinct from every other individual. The particular assemblage of individuals who relate to each other in fairly predictable ways, which are distinct from any other system outside the family, define the family as different from all other families.

The family is characterized by a degree of stability and integration. This does not mean the family is rigid over time, but that one of its properties is a tendency toward equilibrium within a framework of growth, or *morphostasis*. Because the ongoing activities of the family system are organized and integrated in relation to the system itself, each family system tends to establish a relatively consistent life style. Families have characteristic ways of doing, thinking, reacting and growing which tend to distinguish them as unique. Thus, the family puts its personal stamp on each role it plays and each situation it encounters. The family is fairly consistent in regarding others as either honest or untrustworthy, in perceiving life as either exciting or threatening, or perhaps as a constant struggle, in seeking certain experiences and avoiding others.

The family is also characterized by a degree of flexibility and capacity for change. This does not mean the family behaves like a chameleon who constantly changes form in response to environmental shifts. Rather, it refers to the fact that one of its properties is a tendency toward growth within a framework of equilibrium, or *morphogenesis*. Accordingly, families are able to adapt in response to both pressure from within and challenges or perturbations from without.

To the extent that the family either screens out or allows in new information, we refer to it as being either more *open* or more *closed*. The appropriate amount of either openness or closedness can only be decided relative to context. However, when a balance is being maintained, i.e., neither too open nor too closed, we may say that the family is characterized by a state of *negentropy*. By contrast, *entropy* refers to the tendency of a system to move toward chaos or self-destruction, which may occur as a function of being either too open or too closed. In the former case, the family loses its unique identity; in the latter it atrophies in the absence of needed inputs.

A family's typical patterns of behavior are consistent with that family's interpretive system, values and self-definition. A family defines itself and its members according to the metaphors it employs to describe itself in the context of various situations and experiences. And the family's stories about itself and its members participate in the way that reality will be both experienced and created.

When confronted with situations that are not in accord with the family's value system, feedback processes are activated as the system attempts to temper, adapt, minimize or preclude this information. *Positive feedback* indicates that change has occurred and has been accommodated by the system. *Negative feedback* indicates that the status quo is being maintained. The net outcome of these feedback processes is assurance of the continuation of the family's value system as it is manifested in its interaction patterns and in its life style. Indeed, we recognize from the perspective of second-order cybernetics that all feedback is ultimately negative feedback as the system seeks to maintain itself.

If the family system is markedly out of accord with its environment and rejects all inputs, the behavior of the family or its members may conflict with other systems in that environment. Similarly, if the behavior of an individual within the family is markedly out of accord with the family's values and interaction style, the individual may conflict with others within the family. In both cases, there will be pressure to change, to create a more adequate *structural coupling* either between members or between the family and its context.

As family systems function according to the principle of *non-purposeful drift*, they produce outputs deemed to be either useful and/or useless. The criterion of usefulness generally is established by systems outside the family or by the suprasystem. However, problem families, i.e., families poorly adapted to their milieu or whose activities produce individuals who are poorly adapted to their milieu in one respect or another, become "dysfunctional" through the operation of the same basic family development principles that apply to non-problem families.

From their inception, families are engaged in the evolution of a structure which allows and limits what the system can or cannot do. According to the principal of *structural determinism*, we understand that what they do makes sense, or is logical to context. What is more, we recognize that no family attains a perfectly satisfactory or optimal adaptation; all families produce some "error."

However, families are neither "good" nor "bad." They are so labeled by some other system. When the interface of a family with its suprasystem occurs with only tolerable error, the family is said to be reasonably well adjusted. Within the family, when the interface of family members with each other occurs with only tolerable error, the family may view itself and its members as reasonably well adapted. When more than acceptable "error" occurs, and a problem is defined either by family members or by the larger society, the family may present itself for therapy.

The therapist has two options for understanding and working with the family from a systems perspective. She or he may operate from a position as observer (first-order cybernetics) attempting to understand what is going on inside the system. While there is recognition of *recursion*, or the bilateral nature of relationships and mutual influence within the family, there may be no acknowledgment of the way in which his or her presence, approach, perceptions or interventions participate in the creation of the therapeutic reality that emerges. From such a perspective, the therapist takes the role of expert who treats families and works with them according to his or her map or model about how families should be.

On the other hand, the therapist may see him or herself as part of an *autopoietic* whole which includes him or her (second-order cybernetics), recognizing that the observer is part of the observed. In this instance, the therapist understands that every person has a story to tell and that reality is created as a function of each person's story. Thus, we dwell in a *multiverse* of multiple perspectives and there are as many families to be acknowledged as there are family members. Operating according to an *epistemology of participation*, the therapist takes the role of non-expert who co-creates with the clients whatever therapeutic reality emerges. Through a series of mutual *perturbation* and *accommodation* processes change may be facilitated as the therapist works with family members to assist them in the attainment of their goals.

It is our belief that neither position is right or wrong. Families may be helped as the therapist works at the level of either first-order or second-order cybernetics. However, it is our bias that second-order cybernetics enables us to view and interact with clients in a manner which we feel is more respectful of their uniqueness and expertise. Thus, while we draw upon the concepts and models which have been created from and are consistent with the perspective of first-order cybernetics, we utilize them in the context of a postmodern, second-order cybernetics framework.

Chapter 8

A CRITIQUE AND DEFENSE OF THE SYSTEMS PERSPECTIVE

We may never know whether the 'real' world, the ultimate reality which surely underlies all our observations and constitutes our very existence is truly ordered, and if so, whether it is divided into distinct types of special order or manifests one overarching systematic order. What we do know is that the human mind seeks order and that the more general and simple the order it discriminates the more meaning it confers on experience. As long as no direct metaphysical insights into the nature of reality are available, we must reconstruct reality through rational theories with empirical applications.

Ervin Laszlo

The systems perspective would have us see individuals *relatively,* or relative to context, rather than substantively, or as particular types of individuals having particular psychological traits, or being a certain way. Thus Steve is not a specific sort of fellow. Rather, Steve is a certain kind of person with me the way I am with him, or in this context. With a different person, or with me in a different context, Steve is a another kind of person.

Relativism requires that we see reciprocity or circularity in relationships rather than linear cause and effect. The most powerful interpersonal language directs our attention to interfacing rather than to intentionality in one another. That is, "We really get on each other's nerves," replaces, "You always make me angry," or, "You are a rotten person."

Systemic, or relativistic, assessment assumes that the behavior of each defines both the self and the other in a relationship in terms of a given context. When I teach and you attend my lecture we are defined in the context of a classroom as professor and students. We assume reciprocal roles to one another and interact accordingly:

Neither of us could maintain the behaviors logical to these roles for very long in the absence of their logical complement. In other words, I cannot continue to behave, feel and think in a manner appropriate to the role of teacher unless someone takes a reciprocal or complementary role, i.e., feeds back to me through his or her behavior that he/she takes the command implicit in my teaching behavior and responds as a student. The systems model would have us see this reciprocal influence in all social systems, and it suggests that a given role cannot maintain itself of its own energy. Rather, it's maintenance requires another role which is logically complementary to it.

The influence of two persons in a relationship is mutual. Therefore, both share responsibility for whatever is created. While either person may seek to establish unilateral control of the relationship, such efforts are doomed to fail for a relationship is bilateral by definition. As we cannot not communicate, we cannot not influence the relationships of which we are a part. Interdependence is the rule within a systems framework and independence and dependence have meaning only as we redefine them with reference to a given context.

The persons in a relationship are both free and controlled. That is, they are free to the extent that they recognize the limits of the contract that they have evolved with each other. Because of the bilateral nature of the interaction in a relationship, attempts to change the relationship contract are best done by bilateral agreement. While attempts at one-upsmanship are not precluded, they may lead to dissolution of the relationship unless such attempts are transformed into a bilateral effort. When dissolution of a relationship is precluded, as in a parent-child dyad, failure to adjust the context in response to feedback which indicates a problem exists may lead to a continually deteriorating relationship. This is reflected in an increasing frequency and amplification of the behavior that was originally deemed undesirable and was the target for change.

The concepts presented as basic to a systems perspective lay the groundwork for an ecological epistemology. The question of whether the individual or the environment is more powerful is not meaningful in a systems framework. Rather, both are accepted as important elements as the reciprocal relationship between the two is acknowledged. It is assumed that neither can be meaningfully understood without the other. The environment is not viewed as something in opposition to the individual but as inclusive of him or her. The individual is neither the all-powerful self-determining person nor the pawn. Mutual influence is the rule and the interface between individuals and systems provides the key to understanding their relationship.

We believe that the fact that human beings create theories testifies to their genius and uniqueness as the only known organisms who are able to conceptualize their own experience. A systems theory is but one example of this genius. It presents a view of the world in which individuals are seen in a collaborative and cooperative relationship with all other members and aspects of their environment rather than envisioning a world of protagonistic-antagonistic forces.

For us, the systems perspective is a useful explanation of reality. Its generality and applicability to a wide variety of phenomena, however, can be seen as having both assets and liabilities. On the one hand, explanations from this perspective can be so all-encompassing, with concepts so broad, that we are precluded from action. For example, carried to the extreme, a systems perspective would have us see Steve in relation to other persons and systems such as family, peers, work group, church members, etc.,

> who are part of a community system;
> which is part of a societal system;
> which is part of a cultural system;
> which is part of a national system;
> which is part of a world system;
> which is part of the cosmic system;
>
> > of which the viewer is also a part.

When we see the interrelatedness of these several systems, each of which is a part of and to some extent influences and is influenced by the other, we might be led to believe that in order to effectively help Steve we would have to involve ourselves with each of the other systems impinging upon him. Thus, if we take the perspective to its outermost limits, we may be moved to inaction, and possibly to despair. For, a systems perspective can indeed be seen as too general to be useful. However, this generality does not necessarily prevent our taking action. If we are able to focus on those systems which participate most in the maintenance of Steve's problem, then the possibilities for solution assume more manageable proportions.

There seems to be abundant empirical evidence to suggest that the family system exerts the greatest influence on an individual, followed by other systems such as school, church, and work which also have an impact upon the family. These, we maintain, are within the range of our ability to influence as we attempt to help Steve. Further, this does not mean that Steve cannot be helped apart from these systems.

A fundamental premise of the helping professions is that an individual can be helped in a relationship or system with a therapist, and the subsequent change will affect other systems of which that individual is also a member. For example, a change in Steve, if maintained, will have ramifications for his family, work, church, and peer relationships. Because of his new ways of interacting within these systems, Steve's changes will ripple out in a manner not unlike a pebble tossed into a pond. That this can happen is well documented and is in no way inconsistent with systems theory; in fact, it validates this perspective.

From a systems perspective, "mental health" can be seen as relationship health. According to this viewpoint, the therapist's goals include primary prevention activities, or relationship development, in the form of marriage and family development and enrichment, as well as relationship remediation and rehabilitation, or marriage and family therapy. Further, there is an awareness that when viewed in the context of a particular relationship, behavior labeled as "mental illness" may make sense, or may logically fit a given context.

As we draw on the more general systems perspective, we can create a model for a functional system. As is so often the case, the issue seems to be that of achieving a balance between extremes, as illustrated below:

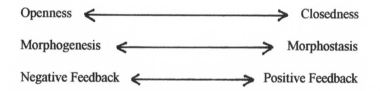

The desired balance between two extremes does not necessarily diminish the value of either extreme as a useful pattern to fit a particular situation. Indeed, a well-functioning set of relationships within a family will contain behaviors that exemplify both extremes. However, over time, the family will tend to blend the two extremes into a balance. Yet a limited balance is probably not sufficient. What probably is essential is the capacity of a family to be able to make decisions to shift or strike a balance at the appropriate time in the appropriate context.

It is our hypothesis that no relationship system can remain effective if it exists for extended periods of time at either end of the continuum. The desired balance is described well in the poem "On Marriage" from *The Prophet* by Kahlil Gibran (1923):

But let there be spaces in your togetherness
And let the winds of the heavens dance between you.

    *   *   *

Love one another, but make not a bond of love:
Let it rather be a moving sea between the shores of your souls.
Fill each other's cup but drink not from one cup.
Give one another of your bread but eat not from the same loaf.
Sing and dance together and be joyous, but let each one of you be alone,
Even as the strings of a lute are alone though they quiver with the same music.
Give your hearts, but not into each other's keeping.
For only the hand of Life can contain your hearts.
And stand together yet not too near together:
For the pillars of the temple stand apart,
And the oak tree and the cypress grow not in each other's shadow.

Thus, we see our task as marriage and family therapists and as family development consultants and parent educators to be that of helping families attain the balance: to be stable and yet be able to change; to be open selectively; to allow for individuation and inclusion; to understand relatedness and interdependence. To know how to decide what to do, when, is the key. A part of this challenge is to teach people to think of their relationships relatively rather than substantively so that they can recognize a basic premise of systems theory, i.e., that one influences while being influenced, that Sue is not a person who "is upset," but that she, "is upset with me the way I am with her" in this particular set of circumstances.

On the other hand, while we accept systems theory as a very useful model and as an applied framework in the field of therapy, we would be remiss if we did not acknowledge that like most theories, it is not without its epistemological problems or paradoxes. For example, three paradoxes in general systems theory have been described by Sadovsky (1974). Such paradoxes concern hierarchy, wholeness and methodology.

The problem of hierarchy involves the paradox of being able to define system "a" as being a component of a larger system "A." This we cannot do unless system "a" can first be defined as a system. Each requires the prior recognition of the other in order for the definition to be valid. As Seidler (1979) notes, there is a mutual interdependence of the two problems, each of which must be solved first in order to solve the other, hence the paradox.

A second paradox rests with the concept of wholeness. In order to be able to describe a system as a whole, we must be able to break it down into parts. Breaking it down into parts requires first that we be able to describe it as a whole. As with hierarchy, ". . . the interdependence of two problems precludes the solution of either, and so of both" (Seidler, 1979, p. 48).

Systems methodology is the subject of the third paradox. As with any discipline, the problem concerns the answer to a chicken and egg question. Did we first have the methodology which enabled us to attain a degree of knowledge based upon which we made certain assumptions? Or, based upon our knowledge of systems did we formulate a methodology which, in turn, is essential to our having that knowledge?

When operating from the level of second-order cybernetics, other problems and paradoxes also arise. For example, Golann, 1988a, 1988b) cautions that attempts, however sincere, on the part of the therapist to assume a non-expert role may paradoxically give him or her greater power. That is, similar to the strategy of going one-down, or owning one's impotence, one gains power by giving it up.

Finally, the whole therapeutic process becomes suspect from a second-order cybernetics perspective. If all behavior fits, or makes sense in context, we are also inconsistent when we proceed to facilitate change, thereby helping people to become misfits within their contexts. What is even more problematic is the awareness that it is not ours to judge what is good or bad, right or wrong. However, as Dell (1983) notes, we do not treat problems. What we treat are deviations relative to our values about how people should be - which takes us into the realm of judgment about good and bad, right and wrong.

Epistemological problems like the paradoxes just described are not unique to the systems model by any means. Paradoxes generated by knowledge claims occur in all theories in all disciplines. For, example, the concept of the unconscious is by definition unknowable within the theory that invents it. Similarly, the empiricist tradition asserts that a knowledge claim is acceptable only through data accessible to our senses. One might ask of this assertion, where is the sensory data that allows this statement as a valid knowledge claim?

We recognize that there are no solutions possible for such epistemological problems given man's inability to transcend himself. And while such problems may render a model no less useful in reality, we feel it is important to point out their existence. Further, while our task as theory-builders is to create a theory that is self-referentially consistent, i.e., does not contain knowledge claims that are contradicted from within by its own constructs, we must not fall into the trap of believing that our theories are greater than they are. We believe it is to the credit of systems theorists that they have recognized the epistemological problems in their model. As Bertalanffy notes:

> The various systems sciences have shown that there are concepts, models and invariants revealing a general order that transcends the more or less special ones in the conventional sciences. Let us be aware that this too is a 'perspective of reality,' determined and limited by our human bondage. But so after all, are also conventional and orthodox disciplines. (1968, p. 145)

Chapter 9

IMPLICATIONS FOR FAMILY THERAPY

> Shifting one's thinking from the individual unit to a social unit of two or more people has certain consequences for a therapist. Not only must the therapist think in different ways about human dilemmas, but he or she must consider himself or herself as a member of the social unit that contains the problem.
>
> Jay Haley

From a systems perspective, the family therapist may be seen as a relationship or context therapist. The focus of his or her expertise is on helping people in marriages, families and other social systems relate to each other in ways that are mutually satisfying. The therapist does not do individual therapy, that is, try to fix a person. Rather, the therapist interacts with clients with an awareness of the context in which problems or symptoms emerged. In an effort to help clients achieve their goals, the therapist facilitates the co-creation of a new context within which the desired behaviors are a logical response.

Family therapy does not require the presence of all family members. The family therapist may work with individuals, or various subsystems as well as with the family as a whole. What is critical is that the interpretive system, or story, which guides the therapist's work defines people relatively, rather than substantively. Thus, family therapy is not about who is in the therapy room. Rather, it is about how the therapist thinks about who is in the therapy room.

From a systems perspective, the therapist views the family as the primary context, with awareness of the other important contexts within which family members live and work. Therefore, systems such as school, work or church are important considerations. Also essential to an awareness of the client context are considerations regarding such factors as gender, race and ethnicity.

Systems theory provides a seminal foundation for relationship or contextual therapy in that two of its underlying assumptions include interdependence and holism. Accordingly, it is assumed that symptomatic behavior such as that generally classified as "madness" or "badness" is logical given its context. Thus, from a first-order cybernetics perspective, the individual pathologies that are described by the psychiatric diagnostic nomenclature are considered to be symptomatic of dysfunctional contexts in which the "dysfunctional" role evolved as a system maintenance or system preservation function.

However, using the same logic, it follows that arbitrarily designating the family as the context for treatment ignores the idea that "family pathology" may be symptomatic of the dysfunction of the suprasystem and may serve a system maintenance function in that larger context. From a second-order cybernetics perspective, it also follows that the therapist must include him or herself in the system. Indeed, as part of the society which defines the client's behavior as dysfunctional, the therapist's role may be a part of the problem (Haley, 1976). If we view family pathology apart from the network of social systems of which the family system is a part, then we have merely moved one social unit higher than "individual pathology."

A general goal of family therapy is to help a context evolve such that symptomatic behavior in an individual is not a necessary role for the continued existence of the system. Community therapy or societal therapy, it would seem, should have a similar goal, i.e., that family pathology is not a necessary role for the continued existence of the society. Thus family, community and societal therapy are of the same class of activities. We as family, community and societal therapists also may be understood as symptomatic of the contexts in which our roles evolved. That is, we are part of the systems we seek to change.

Therapists, therefore, might well be viewed as "bad" or "mad" in the same sense as delinquents or persons with phobias. For we, like other people, cannot transcend ourselves. Whatever theories we invent, they are still our own. This same statement might be made for us and our contexts. While we cannot transcend our contexts, we can be aware that from a systems perspective we participate in the creation of problems through our efforts to help others find solutions.

While the preceding comments might be construed as an indictment of therapists, they are intended as a logical analysis coming from a systems perspective. For good or ill, a society evolves roles to assure the maintenance of that society. Our role as therapists is merely one such role. Our general charge from the society seems to be to help people adapt to the way we want our society to be. This poses an interesting dilemma in that the logic of our model requires us to see that which is called "maladaptive" as making sense. Symptomatic behavior is a functional role in context whether the symptom is "madness" or "badness" in the individual, the family, the community or in the society.

One can infer, from a systems perspective, that if various societal contexts had evolved processes consistent with the ideals set forth by those societies, then therapy *per se* would not be a meaningful or necessary activity. It would seem that a society evolves the role of therapist to deal with discrepancies between its ideals and the processes the society activates to attain these ideals.

For centuries, people have speculated on both the ideal and the processes by which to attain the ideal. Some have thrown up their hands in despair and have sought to break away from society, as witnessed by the various communitarian and utopian experiments that have been attempted throughout history. While setting forth ideals is not necessarily bad, often they are utopian in the sense that the processes we invent to attain them are not capable of being successful. Indeed, as finite beings, we cannot claim infinite wisdom and our inventions will probably always fall short in comparison to our ideals. We can, however, begin to get a closer match between the ideals we pose and the processes we create to attain these ideals.

As therapists, let us not fall into the same trap of implementing methods which contradict what we desire. The therapist whose processes contradict the attainment of the ideal is akin to the spouse who nags as a way of getting more love, or a parent who punishes an adolescent for not being more mature by treating him like a five year old. We must seek to use procedures consistent with the ideals set forth by various models describing well-functioning contexts. And we must help clients formulate goals which are realistic while assisting them in evolving processes by means of which such goals truly are attainable.

Stability and Change

Keeping the above introductory remarks in mind, let us turn now to a closer look at applications for the therapy process which seem to be consistent with a systems perspective. This is an interesting challenge in that generally the systemic framework is viewed as a theory of stability and not a theory of change. It describes quite vividly how a system maintains itself. However, a close look at how a system maintains itself or ceases to exist as a system enables us to describe some general principles to guide our actions as therapists who must be concerned with change.

As described previously, the concept of morphostasis implies a near steady-state within the system. The system has feedback processes which enable the system to recalibrate as necessary in order to maintain itself in this steady-state. Both positive and negative feedback loops are characteristic of all families whether they are labeled as "functional" or "dysfunctional." Thus, whatever a family's current pattern of interaction, it serves to maintain the status quo of the family. However painful an experience may be for family members, there is a certain harmony and security in a given pattern. It fits. It makes sense. It is predictable. Therefore, the persistence of a pattern and a change in pattern need to be considered together. Indeed, two related, useful questions for the family therapist to ask are, "How does this undesirable situation persist?" and, "What is required to change it?" (Watzlawick, Weakland and Fisch, 1974, p. 2).

From a systems perspective, there is no doubt about the appropriate target for change: Change the context, maintain this change, and the family system will gradually adapt to this change. A change in context equals a change in relationship rules. For example, a family's behavior may be different at a formal dinner than it would be at a picnic. How mother and father relate when alone is different from how they relate when one or more family members or others outside the family are present. A change in one person disrupts the family's usual interaction pattern as well. In effect, this change violates the implicit contract about how family members are to be with each other and the whole system seeks new, stable patterns of interaction.

It is important to be aware, however, that the therapist cannot predict the outcome of implementation of the proposition that change in person = change in context = change in family. While positive outcomes may evolve, it is also possible that the system may cease to exist as a family. For example, if one spouse is seen in therapy without the other, the client spouse may make changes that are not acceptable to the other spouse. We therefore may find the other spouse maintaining the interaction pattern which previously was the basis for the identity of the relationship and for each person in the relationship. However, the implicit interpersonal contract would no longer be valid and the new rules for the relationship may not be acceptable. Thus, it is imperative that the therapist be sensitive to the possible repercussions for the whole system of change in any one family member.

At the outset of family therapy, the therapist is the person who is different and who by his or her presence comprises the change in context that is the necessary condition for therapeutic change from a systems perspective. This change in context is a here and now phenomenon for the therapeutic session. The therapist must choose his or her own behavior in the face of attempts by family members to have him or her join the family's pattern and thus to become part of its usual context. With the therapist who behaves differently the family members may experience, understand or begin to behave differently with each other.

If therapy focuses on one person who is identified as a problem without efforts to change the context of the family, changes may be very short-lived. While theoretically the change in the behavior of one person can mean change of the system, the network of relationships, feedback loops, and redundant patterns may be strong enough to offset the impact of a change in the behavior of that person. What is more, from a systems perspective, the problem does not lie within the person. It lies within the system of which the symptomatic behavior is an integral part. The symptomatic behavior is a necessary and logical role in the system.

Stated differently, the symptomatic behavior is "dysfunctional" from another framework or model, but within the interpersonal network of the family, it is a logical, sane response, necessary for the maintenance of the system.   It is, in effect, adaptive in this dysfunctional context.   To focus on changing the individual is to produce behavior that is maladaptive to the family context and thereby threatening to the very existence of the family system.   Becoming functional in terms of the more socially acceptable responses defined by mental health models may not make sense given the symptom bearer's context.   Attempting to change the one without the other would be akin to asking a person to wear blue jeans to a formal dinner or to show love and affection in the face of hostility. Doing this is not impossible, but by definition, behavior that does not fit the context is "crazy."

A systems view suggests that the roles described in the nomenclature of symptomatic behavior as "madness" or "badness" already fit the context. To request change in symptomatic behavior and to leave the context unchanged, by this same definition, asks the person to become crazy. Thus, the therapeutic goal is a change in context which includes the person defined as having a problem. The essence of therapy is to create a context in which symptomatic behavior makes no sense. If the symptomatic behavior persists, by definition, the context has not changed. In the following section we outline some of our thoughts about interventions to facilitate meaningful change. Although we do not point out the distinctions, we have included ideas that are consistent with the perspectives of both first-order cybernetics and second-order cybernetics.

General Principles

1. A family coming to therapy may express a verbal desire to change. It is important to be aware that this verbalization may be part of the family pattern which maintains the status quo. Healthy families probably express no desire to change, but they change spontaneously as appropriate. Stated desires to change can seduce the therapist into believing that this "motivated" family will change more easily than one that reports resistance to change. However, family patterns tend to maintain themselves regardless of expressions to the contrary. For some family members, there may even be an advantage to maintenance of the status quo. There is always a subsystem that benefits from a relationship pattern, regardless of its utility for others. Therefore, through reciprocity, another subsystem is actively participating in maintaining the pattern.

2. The therapist needs to be aware of utopian notions regarding any relationship. Such relationships may look desirable but they probably are not attainable. Total freedom from anxiety, jealousy, fear, worry, and a state of perpetual happiness are decidedly utopian. Both mental health professionals and the popular press participate in sensitizing people to any slight deviation, to the belief that all of life's stresses constitute mental disorders. This, in turn, tends to amplify the frequency and extent of the deviations.

3. What you see is not all there is. The family's actual at home behavior is probably tempered by your presence and by the change in the physical setting. There will be, however, sufficient clues as to the nature of the family's structure and process to allow the therapist to infer what probably happens in the natural setting.

4. Verbal reports of the presenting problem do not give you an accurate picture of the family situation. However, these verbal reports are quite useful as you hear different stories from different people,

giving you a view of each person's interpretive system, primary sensory modalities and metaphors. They are also useful as stimulus events which activate non-verbal and verbal responses between and among family members.

5. The therapist may find it helpful to try to understand how it feels to be a member of a given family in a general way, as well as how it feels to be each member of that family. How each member feels is related to the meaning he or she gives events that occur in the family and what responses are activated in the family system. The therapist might allow him or herself to flow for a while with the family process in order to get a sense of how it feels to be a part of this context.

6. The therapist may find it useful to attend to how family members attempt to "hook" the therapist and thus form a coalition with him or her. Forming coalitions is a logical strategy in families when one member does not feel sufficiently effective in his or her relationship with another member of the family. Each family member may have a pattern of trying to triangulate a third party in an emotional crisis. Thus, "hooking" behavior may be a fairly typical strategy in a given family.

7. Transcending the verbal reports of what family members say they do in response to the symptom bearer, the therapist can predict with reasonable accuracy what the family members actually do by being aware of the usual cultural responses to specific symptoms. What is the cultural response to depression, to delinquency, to hyperactivity, to anxiety, to school failure, or to other behavior problems? These logical, cultural responses are probable in most families. The behavior which logically fits the symptom participates in maintaining and escalating the symptom.

8. A family typically comes in for therapy when one member is manifesting symptoms, usually having been labeled bad or sick. Other family members may appear healthy or normal, perhaps more so in contrast to the symptom bearer. The systems therapist must consider how the symptom bearer's problem is useful to the family; what function it serves; what processes get activated around the symptom bearer; what structure or pattern of interaction maintains the symptom bearer in his or her role as well as others in their roles.

9. The therapist may engage one member of the family in conversation, but it is useful to remember when doing so that other family members are listening as well. The creation of a relationship through conversation with each family member is a perturbation of the system as a whole. In fact, you may want to consider what you desire to have other family members hear or observe. What appears to be individual attention in the context of a family can be quite powerful in affecting all other family members.

10. Most family members want change without having to change themselves, that is, a unilateral change for that which is a bilateral phenomenon. A goal of therapy is to create an awareness of the participation of everyone involved in the creation of both problems and solutions. An example of a useful question in this regard might be to ask parents, "What are you willing to give up in order to achieve the behavior you desire from your child?"

11. The concept of morphostasis refers to a system's ability to restore itself according to its own internal structure and operating procedures following any disturbance to the system, whether from within or without. This natural tendency of the family system can be construed as problematic to a therapist who is, by definition, a perturber of the system. However, it is important to remember that such a natural and healthy tendency of families is a key to the survival of a family. Rather than seeing it as resistance, the therapist must learn to work with this phenomenon. The therapist does so by recognizing that resistance is a relational concept. She or he does not create a problem for the family by asking it to forego a vital survival mechanism, something it probably cannot consciously do. The therapist changes his or her behavior by going with the "resistance," thereby creating a change in context which supports change in the family.

12. From a systems perspective, it may be useful to say that a couple marries, not each other, but each other's family system. The intergenerational interaction patterns are part of the marriage contract, however denied or however much the couple may seek to have their relationship be different. In this sense, to be successful in marriage or family therapy may require change in patterns that extend over several generations.

13. As a systems therapist, you may choose to work with the whole family, an extended family network, or with subsystems of the family. But you are not trying to change one or the other alone. You may work with one or the other as a means of facilitating change in the system. The purest system position is to relate everything to relational significance. You are not really interested in the internal thoughts or experiences of the individual, but you may wish to talk with an individual to learn the significance of thoughts and experiences relative to his or her relationships.

14. A basic rule, from the systems perspective, is that as long as the relationship system keeps interacting around a problem, the problem will be maintained. People cannot talk about the problem unless they have it. Therefore, suspending conversation about a problem may be useful in its solution.

15. Change via systems theory is geared to changing the pattern of the system. Energy directed toward adaptive behavior not only reduces the energy available for maladaptive behavior, but it also provides energy for the system. It is harder to respond negatively in response to a positive behavior than it is to a negative behavior. The therapist might assist family members in expressing their desires in more functional ways.

16. The substantive content of a conversation is probably not where the problem lies. Families often believe that if issues are talked about and resolved, the problems will disappear. From the systems perspective, however, the problem lies in the communication processes and family structure. But the substantive content can be used to facilitate modification or change in the communication processes and structures without expressly discussing either.

17. A key to successful therapy with families is helping the members of the family system realize that they are not independent agents. We are free in our internal experiences but not in our interpersonal exchanges. I can manipulate only my half of the behavior. The actions of each affect the other, thus each person shares responsibility for the actions of the other. Unless you the therapist realize this also, you may have a tendency to mislabel.

18. Many marriage and family problems reflect complementary relationship style exchanges. Complementary behaviors are those

exchanges which are logically opposite: friendly-shy, dominant-submissive, sloppy-clean, etc.   The more complementary the exchanges, the more inflexible the relationship tends to be. Symptoms of complementarity are rigidity and tremendous redundancy. Such exchanges can seduce the therapist into seeing victim-persecutor, or control as residing in one person. From a systems perspective the reciprocal interaction proposition holds that the relationship cannot be maintained as it is unless each continues the complementary role. The understanding by family members that they cannot not behave and cannot not communicate, that they participate in the creation and maintenance of whatever is going on, is essential in marriage and family therapy.

19. Symmetrical relationships describe a competitiveness, which may tend to escalate and ultimately explode, inducing instability. The couple or family members in such a relationship exchange logically similar behaviors. They often see the competitive behavior of the other but do not see themselves as doing similar behavior. A parent who shouts at a child who shouts may not see his or her own behavior as being like that of the child. And if he or she does see it, such behavior may be rationalized on the basis of its having been caused by the other, who shouted first. In an interaction sequence over time, there is no start, although one sequence often is isolated as separate from a previous sequence. "Who started it?" is a misleading and ineffectual question from a systems perspective. It implies linear cause-effect processes.   Reciprocity is the rule and equifinality describes the continuing nature of the pattern.

20. From a systems perspective, the current pattern of interaction within the existing family structure maintains behavior defined as problematic.   The therapist, therefore, may wish to draw upon information about individual and family development in order to have a sense of what might be happening that is more useful behavior given the stages which individual members and the family have already attained at a particular point in time. As each member of the family makes functional, constructive moves toward appropriate developmental tasks, the problem person may no longer be so labeled. The problem behavior will no longer fit the context of the evolving family structure.

21. A systems therapist must ascertain and decide the boundaries of a given family system that are relevant for the purposes of therapy. All persons living together in a household may constitute one definition. However, other persons may play significant roles in maintaining the status quo in a system. If the problem person has been receiving treatment for the presenting problem from a family physician or another therapist for a period of time, or if a significant relationship with another person, such as a friend, or a brother-in-law, has evolved around the problem, the therapist may wish to consider doing the following: He or she may include these persons in therapy and/or seek the input of these persons in attempting to understand the dynamics of the family system. Other significant relationships may be threatened if the problem person gets better. Indeed, it can feel very good to have a "problem" in order to elicit well-intended, sympathetic responses from others. And the responses of others can perpetuate a linear cause-effect interpretive system as they reinforce the labels also used by family members.

22. A major difference between reciprocal and linear cause-effect thinking as regards behavior is reflected in a consideration of whether one asks what behaviors occurred around another, or whether one is concerned with what behavior caused another. From a systems perspective, the issue of concern is the behavior of a family member relative to what preceded it and what followed it. Using linear causality, on the other hand, an ongoing sequence of behavior is arbitrarily divided, with one person's behavior being regarded as the cause of the behavior of the other.

23. "Crazy" is doing something that does not make sense to an observer because it cannot be readily explained. However, "crazy" behavior always fits, or somehow makes sense in context. What is more, doing "crazy" behavior sometimes is the key to change. More specifically, while it does not fit the rules of the system to give a kiss in response to nagging, it probably is more likely to break the pattern than is anger. To the outside observer this does not make sense. To the one doing the kissing, it may make perfect sense if there is an awareness of the reciprocal nature of relationships.

24. We tend to evaluate behavior relative to our notions about what it should be. However, many of these notions, while culturally determined, may be utopian, or at least not useful. A part of family therapy, therefore, may involve helping to change these notions. More useful considerations might include what a given family could be that would be more functional within its culture. A therapist also must consider whether his or her notions, appropriate in his or her culture, are appropriate for a family in its culture.

25. From a systems perspective, problem behavior can be construed as a plea for help. It means the system is not working in the way its members want it to, at least at some level. People with problem behaviors can predict well what will happen in the family, but feel powerless to change what is a self-defeating pattern. Such patterns are interwoven into the fabric of the system and are constrained from change attempts that do not fit the rules of the system. "Crazy" or "abnormal" behaviors may thus be attempts to promote change within the rules of the system.

26. Systems theory suggests that we develop an internal model of how others see us and then we project that onto others. When I speak of someone else, I speak of my perception of that person and my belief about their internal model. Happy people are those who believe that others are going to treat them kindly. Couples who have a strong bond will have a model that allows them to say, "I didn't like that behavior, but I must be doing something to promote it."

27. In well-functioning families, choice fulfillment tends to be spread across members. In families with less than optimal functioning, choice fulfillment tends to be situated in one or two members. Similarly, in well-functioning families, all members are able to be dysfunctional sometimes. In families with less than optimal functioning, one or two persons generally have the honor of getting into trouble all to themselves, helped knowingly or unknowingly by the other family members.

28. Any person can interpret incoming stimuli in different ways if he or she has a flexible interpretive system as opposed to prematurely hardened categories. When family members acquire an alternative explanation or reframe for the behaviors of other family members, different action alternatives become possible. Problem families have

almost reflexive responses, based upon their interpretive systems. These responses are not questioned, perhaps because family members do not have the meta-perspective that many   interpretations are possible.

29.   Family therapy may evolve into parent education or child management training sessions. This probably will not be effective unless one parallels this with parent management training for children. Bilateral change is more likely to evolve into a more basic systemic change. One can, however, use parenting ideas as a means of having an impact on, or perturbing, other aspects of the system, for example, the marital subsystem.

30.   A systems therapist helps families develop stable and consistent leadership; define goals and work toward them in constructive ways by encouragement, cooperation, task completion, nurturance and effective handling of crises; have fun together and have each member learn how to contribute to making happy things happen; develop an interpretive system which allows each to see the reciprocal influence process that occurs when people interface; deal effectively with those institutions outside the family which impinge upon it; anticipate developmental tasks and mobilize the family to help members meet them successfully; rear children who have learned how to build successful families and thus perhaps help toward building more successful families in the next generation.

31.   "Strengths" or "faults" are relative to the interpretive system of the person making the distinction. A strength in one interpretive system may be a fault in another. Thus, the same behavior may be regarded variously as meticulous, clean, picky, ambitious and dedicated, a symptom of workaholism, strong and silent, or dishonest. No behavior has value independent of the interpretive system which so labels it.

32.   The ultimate goal of therapy from a systems perspective is for a couple or family to acquire a more useful epistemology. The fact that a system has requested therapy indicates that the epistemology being used to guide actions and feelings is not effective in achieving desired ends and goals. Thus the therapist attempts to participate in such a manner that a new and more useful set of rules can emerge.

33. A key to successful therapy and to successful relationships is the following: If I am influenced by someone and influence him or her in turn, I can acquire two kinds of freedom in the relationship. I can make choices about how I act toward the other person and I can make choices about how I respond to actions by the other person directed toward me.

34. The therapist listens dispassionately to understand the interpretive system and to ascertain the language the client uses to order his or her experience. This helps him or her to be able select alternative metaphors and frames which may structurally couple with the client. As the therapist also listens passionately, or with empathy, she or he acquires influence and the client becomes more amenable to alternative frames and/or suggested activities. Neither of these stances is mutually exclusive or value free.

35. It may be useful to view a family as many different families, i.e., a different family relative to the many different combinations of members present during a day, a week, or a month There is the family with both parents and all the children present, the family with only dad present while mom is away on business, the family with or without children by previous marriages present. There is also the variety of families as perceived uniquely by each family member.

Engaging the Family, Assessment and Therapeutic Goals

When does therapy begin? By the time a therapist sees a family, it already has begun in two important ways. In the first place, a family with a problem, or with a person identified as having a problem, probably has activated or sought help from others within the family system and/or from without, i.e. from friends, colleagues, teachers, ministers, relatives, etc. Thus the family coming in for therapy probably will already have activated its natural network of resources before seeking professional assistance. The lack of success from these first therapeutic efforts suggests that the input came from an extended family network which was part of the same context as the family system. It was not a source of sufficient difference. Family members often seek such lay therapists. However, by activating its usual network of relationships and staying within its parameters and rules, the context remains the same.

Secondly, therapy with the professional begins the minute contact between the client and therapist is made. The phone call invites the therapist into the family system. As initial information is shared and appointments are scheduled, the therapeutic process is underway. Indeed, how the therapist interacts from the outset influences what is to evolve. The therapist's style and manner on the phone sets the tone for therapy. Similarly, the questions asked, the requirements for who must attend therapy, etc., are all perturbations within the therapy system. For example, the request for all household members to come to the first session is a start at redefining the problem as a family or context problem rather than as an individual problem. The therapist begins the process of co-creatiing with the family a new context.

A therapist also would do well to remember that she or he is a member of the same social context as the family. As an agent implicitly designated by society to assist people in becoming more adaptive in accordance with the expectations of society, the therapist is a member of the family context. However, the therapist is more peripheral and thus has a lessened emotional involvement with the family system. At the same time, therapists are not "objective" in the scientific sense. They are subjective relative both to their theoretical orientation and to the role of therapists in the society of which they are a part. These biases affect the work of the therapist and influence the assessment and goal setting activities of the therapy session.

In the first session, interventions which may be called assessment are part of the therapy. The therapist, as new family member, interfaces with the family, observing, asking questions, listening, making hypothesis testing interventions, etc. The therapist can indirectly intervene into the family under the label of assessment and diagnosis by means of the questions he or she asks. These questions, when not focused on specific prescriptions can creep into a family's consciousness. Such questions and the answers they elicit constitute new input into the family system. For example: Where in your family can you be alone? To whom in your family do you talk to about your problems and successes? How much fun time do you spend with your mom or dad or family? When was the last time you made a funny or surprise thing happen in your family, like putting candles on the table for dinner or bringing home a treat for no reason? In some cases, the answers to these questions are important sources of information. In other cases, the questions can be therapeutic interventions in their own right.

From the outset the therapist interacts with family members in different ways - different from what the clients expect or would have the therapist do. For the therapeutic hour, the therapist joins and becomes a member of the family system. However, in joining, it is imperative that the therapist offer a different way to behave from what the family ordinarily does. The therapist must do behavior that is neither the same nor the opposite of what the family generally does.

This "being different" is not limited to any one particular way. Differentness is relative to context. Dancing at a dance is not different. Dancing at a solemn church ceremony may be different relative to the practices of the church. Differentness is defined here as akin to "craziness," i.e., behavior that does not fit the context. Differentness involves doing behavior that allows family members to be different with one another. It participates in the creation of a new context.

To do what is complementary to the family context is, by definition, neither crazy nor therapeutic. It serves to maintain (with the therapist as a new family member) the existing family context. Any context provides cues as to behavior that is complementary to that context. It is interesting to watch how some families watch for cues (context markers) as to how to be clients in the clinical setting. Therapy-wise clients may begin by coaching the therapist as to how he or she should do therapy.

Indeed, attempts on the part of family members to get the therapist to help them solve problems in the way they already have tried are not unusual. One can describe this as seeking confirmation for their beliefs and validation of their previous efforts to help themselves. Systemically, it is viewed as a morphostatic mechanism essential to the survival of the family. However, for the therapist to do what the family requests, by the above definition, is not therapeutic.

Some therapists may be different, "crazy," from the outset (akin to dancing in the therapy session). Most therapists seem to prefer to gradually influence the creation of change in the family context by selectively complementing and gradually transforming the family's process. The therapeutic ideas and interventions which we will present fit the latter mode rather than the first. Regardless of how the therapist initially engages the family, the goal is to participate in the creation of a different context, one in which stability, flexibility, firmness and nurturance can become a part of the family's pattern.

Assessment from a first-order cybernetics perspective is a process which aims at defining the family's pattern or structure. In effect, it is a "this is what's going on in the system" statement. The labels assigned to individuals using the psychiatric diagnostic nomenclature make no sense, i.e., do not logically fit the model. These individual dysfunction diagnoses do make sense if one uses an individual pathology or medical model.

More frequently than not, however, a single individual is presented as having the problem. It is not unusual to hear from the caller, "Why would you want to see the whole family? It is Joe's problem." If the family has consulted and/or sought treatment from a person whose theoretical orientation involves an individual pathology diagnosis, the belief that the person who needs to be treated and cured is Joe has been reinforced: "If Joe were okay, all would be well." The individual pathology model seems to be the model of choice for many professionals. It is implicit in the label "mental health." The general public, having consumed the services of such professionals over many years, tend to have fairly well internalized this diagnostic framework.

The practitioner of family therapy who bases his practice on the systems model would more accurately be described as a relationship health, a systems health, a family development, or a family health professional: "Thinking of such symptoms as 'depression' or 'phobia' as a contract between people and therefore adaptive to relationships leads to a new way of thinking about therapy" (Haley, 1976, p.2).

Indeed, the assessment of a family is somewhat problematic from the systems perspective. As noted earlier, the definition of what is dysfunctional depends on criteria from outside the context of the system. As we have described, a system which maintains itself evolves roles among its component members to this end. Therefore, in one sense a person with an alcohol problem, a person experiencing depression, a juvenile labeled as delinquent, or an individual with a phobia participate in feedback loops between family members by which the system is maintained. However, in the broader society, these roles are viewed as not useful, or as waste products of the family system. A challenge for the family therapist is to help the family maintain itself without roles judged by society to be maladaptive.

In a general sense, the nature of the presenting problem is not specific as to the pattern of interaction or structure of the family. Whether the person identified as having a problem is called alcoholic, depressed, delinquent or phobic, tells you little about the pattern of interaction within which the problem is being maintained. Systems theory provides no explanation as to the different kinds of roles that may emerge in a family context.

Defining a "negative" pattern in a family implies the flip side of the coin, or an inference about what a healthy or "positive" family pattern looks like. While it is useful to know the existing pattern, the diagnosis of dysfunction by either the therapist or family members implies that the therapist or the family members have a model in their heads about what a functional family looks like. To a great degree, these models reflect the values of the community and social context of which the family is a member.

Specific family therapies describe functional families in a variety of ways. Our concern is the use of a systems perspective to derive a picture of a well-functioning family system. A few propositions and related questions which focus on desired processes are presented below:

1. *A system needs to be stable and yet be able to change or to be flexible.* How is stability maintained in a given family? How does change occur? Are family interactions consistent, thus providing the security of predictability?

2. *Families, like individuals, go through developmental stages.* At what stage is the family? At what stage is each individual member of the family? At what stage did the crisis begin?

3. *The family needs to be both open and closed.* How open is the family from within and without the system? Under what circumstances and through what processes does it become open to influences or capable of shutting down influences? What value orientation or explanation justifies this decision?

4. *Family members need to be individuals and yet feel like they belong.* How is individuality respected? How are attempts at inclusion and togetherness handled? Do family members have independence of thoughts, feelings, and judgment? Does the family seek to promote giving up a sense of self in favor of the family identity?

5. *Communication is feedback and this information exchange is the energy that maintains the system.* How much energy is directed toward maintenance functions? Toward task functions? How do family members learn about their behavior? What are the feedback mechanisms in the family? Are messages clear? Ambiguous?

6. *A system is composed of subsystems with roles which logically complement each other.* Are these roles clear? Are these roles confused and conflicted? Is the parental subsystem marked by clear generational role differences? Do children parent? Do parents rely on children for emotional support? Is the parental subsystem dependent upon grandparents?

Our bias towards second-order cybernetics suggests that assessment is most useful when it describes what needs to happen in the family, what is desired, rather than what's wrong with the family. As stated earlier, these are related statements since the flip side of "what's wrong" is the complementary "here is what would be right" or "this is the way we would like things to be." The way one thinks about a problem and labels it can crystallize the problem and aid in its persistence. Assessment which helps a family decide a direction for therapy transforms the therapy experience into a developmental process in which the family members learn to be different with one another in the different context co-created with the therapist.

The following general characteristics seem to be keys to the successful functioning of family systems and help define "what would be right" processes:

1. A legitimate source of authority, established and supported over time.

2. A stable rule system established and consistently acted upon.

3. Stable and consistent shares of nurturing behavior.

4. Effective and stable child rearing and marriage maintenance practices.

5. A set of goals toward which the family and each individual works.

6. Sufficient flexibility and adaptability to accommodate normal developmental challenges as well as unexpected crises.

More specific information regarding the family members' goals for themselves may be gathered by asking them how they would know that therapy had been successful. While clients usually are very good at describing what they don't like, what is problematic, they generally have difficulty articulating what they would like. The therapist may assist this process by asking clients to consider what would be going on if things were the way they would like them to be. More specifically, they may ask some version of the "miracle question" presented below:

> Suppose that one night there is a miracle and while you were sleeping the problem that brought you to therapy is solved: How would you know? What would be different?

What will you notice different the next morning that will tell you that there has been a miracle? What will your spouse notice? (de Shazer, 1991, p. 113)

The family's designation of one person as "the problem" may be for purposes of public consumption. Many family members can assess and are aware of other problems which family rules prohibit them from sharing publicly. Thus it is important to remember that from a systems perspective the verbal messages about a problem are most helpful as labels or metaphors which provide information regarding interaction patterns within the family system. For example, a child described as a "monster" or as "sensitive" implies behaviors that complement these categories. One can infer from such labels the kinds of relationships which exist between parents relative to the child in question.

The systems perspective suggests that we focus on here and now processes as the necessary and sufficient data for assessment (equifinality), and for the creation of therapeutic goals. Here and now questions the therapist may find useful in observing the family include the following: How do family members sit relative to one another? Who speaks? To whom? In what sequence? What nonverbal messages do you observe with what specific activities?

Therapy can be viewed as a process which involves helping the family move, through a series of incremental steps, toward a basic goal: the gradual transformation of the context into one in which symptomatic behavior is no longer a complementary role. In the following section we present ideas and/or specific interventions which might be utilized to facilitate the process of change.

Pragmatics

1. Very few families come to therapy with a systems epistemology as part of their implicit or explicit interpretive frames. They may acknowledge that each person affects the other, but generally they will ask the therapist, either directly or indirectly, to join them in their effort to help or change the symptom-bearer. When an attempt is made to have the family become involved in the problem, they may

choose to withdraw from therapy and search for someone who will "treat" the family member identified as having the problem. As a means of involving the entire family in what the systems therapist believes is a family problem, the therapist may need to appear to join the family in its efforts to change the symptom-bearer.

2. Helping everyone become a part of the problem is not necessarily equated with having everyone admit to being a part of the problem. It does mean perturbing the communication processes or structure of the family in such a way that all of the members are included, at least implicitly: "You tell me that Johnny's hyperactivity is the problem. I wonder how he was selected instead of Joan, for her weight; instead of Mom, for her anxiety and feelings of isolation; instead of Dad, for his tendency to overwork and reluctance to come home?"

3. Circular questions enable the therapist to help family members see how their behaviors with one another are connected. For example, the therapist may ask the child, "What do you have to do in order to get Mom to yell at you?" Or, one parent may be asked how she or he would describe the reaction of the other parent to problem behavior on the part of a child. The focus thus shifts from specific behavior to relationships and to the impact of responses to behavior.

4. Problems are often viewed as active agents which must be attacked. All we may need to do, however, is to help remove inhibitors which prevent improvement or resolution. Human behavior may be understood as a stream that needs to be unblocked, so that it may flow more freely. Any different response other than the logical "attack" may break the log jam. For example, a family with a long history of problems may not have experienced happy events for a long time. A prescription for doing "silly" or "crazy" things may unlock resources and provide renewed energy for coping with problems.

5. A crucial task for the therapist is to help clients articulate their goals. However, while they may be very proficient at describing problems, or what they don't like, they may find it more difficult to describe solutions or what they would like. And general global statements about what they desire or would like to have others do have a low probability of being attained. For example, the family member

may express a desire to be happy. In response, the therapist might request that the client describe what would be going on if he or she were happier. Similarly, it is essential to have clients break down requests for "more loving" or "more caring" behavior into precise behavioral descriptions of what this means: For example, "She would give me a back rub," or "He would call when he is going to be late."

6. Many families believe they have little to talk about except problems. A therapist might help the family enrich its repertoire of experiences by suggesting that they go to a movie, a play, out to dinner, or visit the zoo, etc., in order to get new inputs into the system and provide something different about which to talk. Sharing and self-disclosure by family members also may increase the amount of positive information available to the family for discussion.

7. A happy family is one in which happy things happen. A useful consideration is how many things family members do for fun, and whether they always take parenting, marriaging, and familying seriously. Correspondingly, how much time do mom and dad spend doing fun things together as husband and wife, apart from the children? Many couples forget how important it is to be husband and wife as well as parents. Good marriages create a context for well-functioning families.

8. One of the most useful ways to understand the overall patterns in a family may be to ask one of the members to describe a typical day in the life of the family, beginning with when the first person gets up and ending when the last person goes to bed. The therapist may quickly learn about such things as whether children are getting up on their own, whether meals are eaten together, how bedtimes are handled, etc. Given this information, suggestions may be made for altering routines, thus facilitating a shift in context as old patterns are interrupted and new behaviors occur.

9. A systems therapist realizes that children are very sensitive to their parents. If parents communicate by their actions that they love each other and their marriage, the children will respond to this. If parents are optimistic, it is likely that the children will also be optimistic. Families that are having difficulties generally do not communicate optimism and hope. There must be a steadfastness in the application of positive pressure. Problems must be met, addressed,

dealt with effectively, and without blaming. That is, problems are discussed sufficiently to understand what is going on. Then the effort is aimed at finding solutions rather than toward a continued rehashing of what went wrong.

10. It is important to participate in the creation of conditions within a family which foster and enhance individual self-esteem. There must be stable, consistent leadership by the parents and an emphasis on constructive behavior. Using these as a foundation, a family can then build toward good work habits, cooperation, and task completion. In a family experiencing severe problems, generally there will be little that is done together. Tasks are not completed. It is likely that the family will not be very well liked by its members. Are there tasks that get done by the family? Is everything done in a haphazard manner? Good feelings and self-esteem come from productivity. If the ability to do things well is not developed, there may well be problems.

11. An important rule for the systems therapist is to help bring expectations into focus. Ask where family members are going rather than focusing on where they don't want to be. For example, it probably is not productive only to give a child many "don'ts" and then to punish him or her when a rule is broken. The child must have a goal on which to focus. Similarly, for one spouse to nag another for nagging probably is not going to be productive. The emphasis should be on where and how things should be rather than on how things go wrong. The family may benefit from the practice of feedforward messages, or learning to request the desired behavior rather than criticizing the undesirable behavior. Feedforward messages not only introduce a possibly more effective behavior, they also provides vivid descriptions, probably specific and behavioral, about what is desired. Thus the criticism, "You never hug me!" becomes, "I would really like a hug."

12. The absence of negative, destructive elements is not the same as the presence of positive, constructive elements. If you treat a person as she or he is, that person probably will continue the same old behavior patterns. If you treat a person as he or she could be, there is an increased possibility for change. For example, the therapist helps

the family   recognize that dealing with an adolescent effectively requires attention to the things the teen could and should be. Stopping delinquent behavior through punishment is not the same as generating something creative and useful. The former relates to the person as he or she is, the latter moves toward potential.

13.   It may be useful to help family members shift from a discussion of a particular topic, to a discussion about how they talk with one another, relate to each other, handle problem-solving, make decisions, etc. The topic then becomes the process. Although they may attempt to discuss even the process with some of their same conflictual interpersonal behavior patterns, the therapist may assist them in learning a constructive way of meta-communicating. This can be done through role-playing, modeling, practicing or having the therapist take the role of the alter ego and coaching family members as they talk.

14.   A key aspect in learning a new process may be learning to describe relatively or relationally rather than substantively. When you do, I do and I feel, and then you do and you seem to feel, etc., rather than, "You made me mad," or, "If only you would...".   This is fundamental to learning to meta-communicate, or learning to talk about how one interacts.

15. People in relationships experienced as problematic tend to pay more attention to nonverbal than to verbal communication.   This sensitivity to analog often precludes resolution of the issue or problem. For example, if Johnny, upon being told that it is time for bed, decides to pout and talk back, and the parent responds with, "Don't talk to me like that," or else pleads with or placates the child, this response to the analog assures its continuation.   A response to task or issue, by-passing the analog, probably will be a more useful response.   The therapist might help family members focus on issues rather than being sidetracked by attitude.

16.   What must family members believe or assume about themselves and others to maintain the behavior that follows logically from their beliefs and sustains their dysfunctional patterns?   What other metaphors would help them to make different choices?   A therapeutic task may be to provide the family with explanations, or reframes, which provide solutions where their existing interpretive

systems do not. Such an alternative explanation probably needs to be of a higher logical order than the family's existing interpretive system. That is, it must transcend the dichotomies currently employed by the family. For example, within a framework which says obedience = good, and disobedience = bad, rebellious behavior by a teenager might be reframed as normal movement toward independence or as serving a function to give mother a role: "Johnny is the last child to look out for you and be sure that you still have your job in the family." To the teenager the reframe might be: "It is really generous of you, as the last child, to look out for mother and be sure that she keeps her job in your family." The goal of the reframe is to provide an interpretation that explains the interaction sequence as well as, if not better than, the previous explanation. A new interpretation opens up behavioral alternatives and hopefully precludes existing behaviors which the family does not find useful.

17. Many problems in families would resolve themselves if it were not for the triangulation process, or the formulation of coalitions in an attempt to gain more power. The intervention of a third party may look like a rescue attempt, but it can also be construed as blocking resolution. For example, two children who fight, often begin to fight less when mom or dad stops intervening to break up fights. The relationship is thus free to seek its own level, to build its own pattern with different responses without the triangulated third party. Similarly, parents might be encouraged to let one another deal with a child rather than becoming the third leg of a triangle.

18. The therapist may help family members defuse and realign triangles by inviting them to tell each family member what every other family member is telling you about them. For example, "Jill, let me tell you what Matt told me about you." "Matt, let me tell you what Jill told me about you." Of course, Matt and Jill may coalesce around the person doing the sharing, but if everyone agrees to participate, the "game" is out in the open.

19. A family therapist might assist a family in learning to think relatively, thus seeing directly or indirectly, the self and relationship defeating patterns in which each member of the family is engaged. The general rule is that no behavior can be maintained for long on its

own energy; it needs a complementary behavior to maintain it. Criticism logically begets and maintains criticism. Shouting logically begets and maintains shouting or withdrawal - a louder form of shouting. As a therapist, it is important to remember that the road to change is via a change in context, or new behavior, the logical response to which is the behavior desired. An empathic, respectful, understanding response in the face of shouting, if maintained, will slowly but surely bring down the shouting. Rather than simply reacting, family members may benefit from learning to choose their own behavior in response to others.

20.   In an interaction sequence between family members, a therapist might interrupt to help any member choose a response different from what is characteristic in that sequence and thus participates in maintaining it. A different response will break the self-defeating reciprocal pattern. Such different responses may not seem logical to the given event; in fact, they may appear to be "crazy." But they make sense in that they break the pattern and introduce something different. This is one instance in which craziness may be seen as a logical, or sane, response to dysfunctional communication.

21.   Change in behavior in a family member is no change if it is the opposite of the problem behavior. A family member, in response to the ineffectiveness of shouting, may withdraw and become silent. This appears to be "different" behavior. However, silence is the opposite identity member of noise (shouting), and withdrawal is the opposite identity member of presence. Thus silent withdrawal is a louder form of shouting and therefore, by definition, is not "different." To do something different would be, for example, for one member of the shouting match to tickle the nose of the other with a feather, thereby stepping out of the linear, logical response pattern.

22.   Providing families with insight about how they function is of questionable value from a systems perspective. Clients will tend to discuss these therapist-given insights using the same dysfunctional patterns they employ to process problematic issues. They may even find pieces of the insight to use, or form a coalition with, to justify their position. Thus the substantive explanation is of limited utility in changing behavior. The nature of relationships may need to change,

but awareness must be accompanied by a new process. And a new pattern of interaction can be initiated without insight.

23. One of the most frequent types of parent combination in families experiencing problems is a couple composed of one who is weak and one who is strong. This complementarity often creates a spiral effect, which further isolates the parents from each other and makes their treatment of the children even more divergent. The parental coalition needs to be strengthened so that the child is treated according to the child's needs and not according to the parents' needs. Parents may be encouraged to coalesce around their parental rules and discipline and to share the functions of both nurturer and enforcer.

24. *Quid pro quo,* or something for something else negotiations, i.e., "If I do this then you will do that," can be useful in resolving conflict in specific areas of disagreement such as in-laws, money, social behavior, and child rearing. When there is an outcome or a task to perform, such negotiations tend to work well. But *quid pro quo* behavior generally does not work well with relationship-focused problems: "I'll give you three hugs in return for two back-rubs." If you trade-off interpersonal behavior, you are no longer able to be spontaneous. Feeling choice in this area is essential, and the tally chart must be thrown away. Many people acquiesce in doing loving behavior that is requested. However, its having been requested removes the possibility of acting freely in the matter. And to comply under such conditions may lead to a feeling by the other such as, "Yes, but I had to ask you."

25. In a family, the person exercising what looks to be power behavior, i.e., the authoritarian, has the least actual control. In effect, one gets more control by giving up control. A relationship which allows control to shift back and forth is probably experienced as stronger. Control behavior, as manifested in the parallel relationship style, is reciprocally controlling and seems to have built into it the implicit understanding that actual control of a relationship is not possible, or is shared. Control as well as freedom for both parties are possible when both recognize and accept the reciprocal nature of relationships.

26. In a well-functioning system, it is validating for all of the members to see themselves as making choices and thus as being powerful and having an impact on the system. Each family member needs validating experiences, or opportunities to make decisions which affect the others. If they are not given, they will be taken, often in ways not valued by the family.

27. Families often confuse or mix requests for behavior or performance with the request to feel a certain way. The statement, "I, or you, should feel or should not feel...," is an example of the "be spontaneous" paradox. It is one thing to request performance (take out the garbage), but quite another to request enjoying it (and like it).

28. In a well-functioning relationship, both parties can entertain two contradictory ideas at the same time. "I can understand the world as you see it and also as I experience it." This requires a meta-perspective of theoretical relativity with the overriding view that there is no "true" explanation (mine) and no "false" explanation (yours).

29. Many chronic family problems have developed in response to crises, i.e., illness, loss of a job, etc. The crisis occurred and the family adjusted, but when the crisis ended, the pattern was never dropped. For example, father becomes ill. Family adjusts. Mother goes back to work and children assist with family chores. Father gets well, but the "crisis" pattern persists without appropriate adjustments and the family feels stuck. This same tendency can be used to help the family become unstuck, as a therapist participates in inducing a new "crisis." For example, the therapist may assign a family member the task of developing relationships in other contexts outside the family. New inputs or energy will thus be brought into the system and role changes will be necessitated as the member's behavior changes.

30. As with all living systems, the family's survival is extremely bound up with its external environment. As family members fit the family context, so the family system fits the context of the system of which it is a subsystem. It must constantly adapt to and/or exert influence upon its environment. Some families feel powerless in the face of environmental pressures. Indeed there are some environmental pressures about which a single family cannot do very much, such as government policies. However, the therapist may find it useful to help families learn to have an impact where possible. How can the

work schedules of both parents be modified so that at least one is home with the children and so that both are in the home together for at least a short time if this is an acceptable or desired change?

31. People outside the family unit affect the family and can reinforce its patterns in ways that are either helpful or not helpful. If a child has a problem doing homework, there will be an additional flow of negative information coming to the family from the school. The systems therapist, making an ecological intervention, would consider calling the teacher and suggesting that instead of only the steady stream of complaints, he or she also try to compliment the child and send home notes indicating when positive behaviors have occurred. Hopefully, this would influence the nature of the interactions within the family. Other such ecological interventions might include talking with a coach, boss, peers as appropriate, and/or getting these different influence people together independently of the person defined as having a problem or the family. The key element for which to look is the source of support for the problem person in the face of a network of negative interaction patterns.

32. It may be useful to request that family members not discuss their problems with persons outside the family, at least during the course of therapy. As coalitions and triangles may be formed within, so they also be created through conversations with persons from without. And while the intentions of friends may be sincere and their efforts to offer advice and help well-intentioned, a two against one situation may be created, thus undermining the process. Therefore, the establishment of a boundary around a relationship or around the family will probably be more useful until the desired goals have been attained. Once therapy has ended, clients also may recognize the utility of maintaining such a boundary even when things are going well.

33. Just as family members often see themselves as independent agents, therapists may see themselves as independent of their clients. However, whatever is created is created together, whether in the family or in therapy. As we label clients as "unmotivated," "not willing to change" or "resistant," we are labeling ourselves. The challenge becomes one of recognizing our participation, or seeing ourselves

relationally: "How can I behave with this client in such a manner that motivation, or willingness to change, or being receptive are logical responses?"

34.   What doesn't happen in therapy provides as much useful information as what does. When a therapist assigns an activity to be completed outside therapy, the client may or may not "comply." Rather than labeling the client "non-compliant," there are many other stories the therapist can tell him or herself. Perhaps this response on the part of the client was appropriate boundary maintenance behavior. Perhaps it was an inappropriate suggestion on the part or the therapist, or perhaps the timing was off. Perhaps, had the therapist phrased the suggestion differently, it might have been accepted more readily.

35.   What the therapist chooses to introduce as a topic of conversation or to avoid discussing has a significant impact on the unfolding of the therapy process. It is imperative for the therapist to be sensitive to the impact of the choice to focus or not on such issues as gender and the related area of power distribution in the family; religion and spirituality and the relative importance of such a belief system for the family; the impact of race and culture on the client's ability to function successfully; socioeconomic and other resources available to the client. The therapist also needs to be sensitive to and reflect upon the stories she or he is telling her or himself about the client, about the clients' stories, about the therapy process. Are my stories the most useful for this client system in this situation? What other kinds of stories could I be telling myself? Are there stories that would be more effective in helping these clients achieve their goals? How would therapy have evolved differently if I had been telling myself different stories? Have I considered asking the clients what they are telling themselves about therapy?

Final Thoughts

One of the criticisms of systems theory is that it does not describe change mechanisms more precisely. One can illustrate such criticism as follows: "Okay, so you change the context and this change in context = change in family. But you do not explain with the precision of, for example, behavior theory, how such change is to be accomplished."

Generally, such criticism comes from the more traditional, reductionistic philosophy of the behavioral sciences. Accordingly, we are told to break things down into their component parts, learn as much as possible about these components independent of one another, and the total of the bits of information will give us the knowledge necessary to understand, predict and control our world. And while criticism coming from a reductionistic framework is legitimate within that framework, it is based upon a set of assumptions different from those underlying systems theory. Systems theory is anti-reductionistic. To study component parts out of the context of other parts is not meaningful, for each is different without the other. Systems theory provides us with an holistic perspective. And while at one level the systems framework is a meta-theory, at another level, it is also a pragmatic theory which specifies the mechanisms of change in a holistic way, eschewing reductionism as inconsistent with its basic premises.

Systems theory as a meta-framework is a unifying model, and many traditional therapeutic processes, e.g., analytic, affective, behavioral, and cognitive, are readily accommodated within its parameters. The systems perspective would enable us to describe each such approach as merely one way in which to create a different context for facilitating the transformation of a family system. Thus specific family therapies, such as those of Satir, Whitaker, Bowen, Ackerman, Haley, Patterson, Watzlawick, and others, may draw upon aspects of many of the more traditional therapies. What the family therapists have in common is a meta-perspective of seeing the interrelatedness of people and systems.

As one moves to the level of second-order cybernetics, systems theory also provides a framework for ethical behavior as the therapist understands the degree to which she or he may participate not only in the attainment of solutions but also in the creation of problems. The observer is part of the observed, the therapist is part of the therapy system. Reality is created as a function of the stories we tell ourselves. Awareness of the ability each of us has to create reality, and to influence the realities created by others for themselves, calls us to act on this awareness. Recognition of our interdependence and the fact that we are all involved in each other's destiny requires behavior that is respectful, valuing and worthy of all, individuals as well as the whole.

Chapter 10

IN CONCLUSION

Having abandoned the vocabulary of minds and other minds and thus of intersubjectivity, having rejected a commitment to a single objective reality variously apprehended from a variety of subjective viewpoints, our understanding of man is changed. What is in question is not merely a vocabulary, not merely a set of concepts, but a way of comprehending not a single reality, but the multiple realities represented by sometimes shared, sometimes divergent subject matters and the subjects they serve to identify.

Steven Bartlett

And so the book is finished, and yet it is never really finished or complete. Whenever one asserts what one knows, one is already different, having learned from the very assertion of one's knowledge. And we have learned from the preparation and revision of this manuscript, just as we hope that you have learned from reading the fruits of our effort. You were very much with us as we wrote - you the student of social work, family therapy, counseling, counseling psychology, and ministry, as well as you the practitioner involved in working with families. We tried to anticipate your questions and provide answers. But you were a very large and diverse audience and we feel sure there were many questions which you may have which we have left unanswered. However, as stated in the introduction to this book, your challenge is to continue to learn on your own and to develop your own systems perspective if this seems to be a useful model for you in your life and work. It certainly has been useful to us. And among other things, it continues to challenge us to learn more about disciplines which previously seemed remote from our formal study of people and human behavior.

We have learned that knowledge is not necessarily ordered in the way that college and university departments are organized. The systems perspective as thus developed seeks to be a unifying theory, or meta-theory, which transcends the specific theories in disciplines that without a unifying framework appear separate and distinct. For us, the interdependence and complementarity which we describe between people and systems also applies to theories and academic disciplines.

Further, we no longer regard it meaningful to say that a theoretical framework is either true or false. We do not believe that the truth of falseness of a theory can be known to us. Even if true, we cannot know that it is true in an absolute sense. We can only evaluate the usefulness of a theory relative to the reasons for which we create, adopt or implement it in practice.

We believe that rather than speaking of theories, it is more useful to speak of stories. This reminds us that we all have our perceptions of reality and that each person's perception is valid or meaningful for that person. It also reminds us that reality is not separate from us, but is our creation as a function of our beliefs and the behaviors based on these beliefs.

Finally, we would like to close with what we consider to be a major challenge of a systems perspective. For in the process of writing and again in rewriting this book we have become painfully aware of the difficulties involved in using a language system which is premised on linear concepts to describe adequately a model which assumes mutual interaction and contextual relativity. Thus the challenge for all of us who find systems theory a useful map for the territory we would traverse is to define a symbol system consistent with that map, a key that will better enable us to make use of the map. Undoubtedly such a key would also help us to unlock the doors to a greater understanding and knowledge of the territory we describe as family therapy.

REFERENCES

Barnhill, L., & Longo, D. (1978). Fixation and regression in the family life cycle. *Family Process, 17*, 469-478.

Bartlett, S. (1977). Unpublished manuscript. St.Louis University, St.Louis, MO.

Bateson, G. (1972). *Steps to an ecology of mind.* New York: Ballantine.

Becvar, D., & Becvar, R. (1993). *Family therapy: A systemic integration.* Boston, MA: Allyn & Bacon.

Becvar, D., & Becvar, R. (1996). *Family therapy: A systemic integration.* Boston, MA: Allyn and Bacon.

Bender, A. (1976). Unpublished manuscript. St. Louis, MO: St. Louis University.

Berrien, F. (1968). *General and social systems.* New Brunswick, N. J.: Rutgers University Press.

Bertalanffy, L. von (1968). *General system theory.* New York: George Braziller.

Bossard, J. (1945). The law of family interaction. *American Journal of Sociology*, pp.292-294.

Bowen, M. (1976). Theory in the practice of psychotherapy. In P. J. Guerin, (Ed.), *Family therapy: Theory and practice* (pp. 42-90). New York: Gardner Press.

Brand, S. (1974). *II Cybernetic frontiers.* New York: Random House.

Bronowski, J. (1978). *The origins of knowledge and imagination.* New Haven, CT: Yale University Press.

Carter, E., & McGoldrick, M. (1980). *The family life cycle: A framework for family therapy.* New York: Gardner.

de Shazer, S. (1991). *Putting difference to work.* New York: W. W. Norton.

Dell, P. (1983). From pathology to ethics. *Family Therapy Networker, 1,* 29-64.

Duvall, E. (1962). *Family Development.* Philadelphia: Lippincott.

Erickson, E. (1963). *Childhood and society.* New York: W. W. Norton.

Foucault, M. (1979). *Discipline and punish: The birth of the prison.* New York: Pantheon.

Gergen, K. (1991). *The saturated self.* New York: Basic Books.

Gibran, K. (1951). *The prophet.* New York: Alfred A. Knopf.

Golann, S. (1988a). On second-order family therapy. *Family Process, 27,* 51-65.

Golann, S. (1988b). Who replies first? A reply to Hoffman. *Family Process, 27,* 68-71.

Haley, J. (1963). *Strategies of psychotherapy.* New York: Grune & Stratton.

Haley, J. (1973). *Uncommon therapy.* New York: W. W. Norton.

Haley, J. (1976). *Problem-solving therapy.* San Francisco, CA: Jossey-Bass.

Harper, J., Scoresby, A., & Boyce, W. (1977). The logical levels of complementary, symmetrical and parallel interaction classes in family dyads. *Family Process, 16,* 199-210.

Hill, R., & Rodgers, R. H. (1964). The developmental approach. In H. Christensen (Ed.), *Handbook of marriage and family therapy.* Chicago: Rand Mcnally.

Howard, G. (1991). Culture tales. *American Psychologist, 46,* 187-197.

Ichheiser, G. (1949). Misunderstandings in human-relations: A study in false social perception. *American Journal of Sociology, 54,* 400-401.

Keeney, B. P. (1983). *Aesthetics of change.* New York: Guilford Press.

Kelly, G. (1955). *The psychology of personal constructs* (Vol. I). New York: W. W. Norton.

Kuhn, T. (1970). *The structure of scientific revolutions.* Chicago: University of Chicago Press.

Laszlo, E. (1972). Basic concepts of systems philosophy. *Systematics, 10,* 40-54.

Mair, M. (1988). Psychology as storytelling. *International Journal of Personal Construct Psychology, 1,* 125-138.

Malcolm, J. (1978). The reporter at large: The one-way mirror. *NewYorker,* May 15, pp. 39-114.

122   *Systems Theory and Family Therapy: A Primer*

Maturana, H. R., & Varela, F. J. (1992). *The tree of knowledge.* Boston, MA: Shambhala.

McNamee, S., & Gergen, K. (1992). Introduction. In S. McNamee & K. Gergen, (Eds.), *Therapy as social construction* (pp. 1-6). Newbury Park, CA: Sage.

Palazzoli, R., Boscolo, L., Cecchin, G., & Prata, G. (1978). *Paradox and counterparadox.* New York: Jason Aronson.

Sadovsky, V. N. (1974). Problems of general systems theory as a meta-theory. *Ratio,* pp. 33-50.

Scoresby, A., & Christensen, B. (1976). Differences in interaction and environmental conditions of client and non-client families: Implications for counselors. *Journal of Marriage and Family Counseling, 2,* 63-72.

Seidler, M. (1979). Problems of systems epistemology. *International Philosophical Quarterly, 19,* 29-60.

Speer, C. (1970). Family systems: Morphogenesis and morphostasis, or is homeostasis enough? *Family Process, 9* (3), 259-277.

Watts, A. (1972). *The book: On the taboo against knowing who you are.* New York: Vintage.

Watzlawick, P. (1976). *How real is real?* New York: Vintage Books.

Watzlawick, P., Beavin, J., & Jackson, D. (1967). *Pragmatics of human communication.* New York: W. W. Norton.

Watzlawick, P., Weakland, J., & Fisch, R. (1974). *Change: Principles of problem formation and problem resolution.* New York: W. W. Norton.

White, M., & Epston, D. (1990). *Narrative means to therapeutic ends*. New York: W. W. Norton.

Whitehead, A. N. (1926). *Science and the modern world*. New York: MacMillan.

Index